The Four Pillars of the Kingdom

Joe Brooks

This book is dedicated to my wife, Amber, who has been my biggest fan, my inspiration and continues to be the greatest gift that God could have given me in this world.

Table of Contents

Learn - He Wants Us to Know Him

Live - He Expects Us to Live by His Example

Love - He Wants Us to Take His Message to the World

Introduction

John 3:16 For God so loved the world, He gave His only begotten son, that whosoever believeth in Him shall not perish, but have everlasting life.

An Institutional Faith

Let me say right up front that as a writer and as a Christian, I make no pretence to breaking new ground here. This is intentional. Too often in matters of faith "new ground" is synonymous with heresy. People propose a "new" way of approaching the Bible that ends up straying from the text altogether. What I propose is to engage those fellow believers who might not have taken the time to truly consider why they are believers. You know who you are! Christians who were simply born into their faith the way that many of us are born with one parent's blue eyes or the other parent's cleft chin. There is nothing

8

wrong with that, by the way. Can you think of a greater birthright than to inherit, by their example, your parents' love of Christ? Of course, I am not saying that you can have salvation passed down to you through your parent's genetic code, but parents who serve the Lord create a fertile ground for the young soul to grow. They can help to spread what C.S. Lewis calls the "good infection" of Christ.

However, as we grow older, there comes a time when we should ask ourselves why we believe what we believe. There comes a time when you should step out and it becomes **your** faith, **your** relationship with Christ, not just an inheritance. Then, when it is yours, you can "pass it on" to the next generation by being an example of Christ's love to your children, to your friends and to your neighbors. However, should that next generation (or even members of your own) come to you and ask "why," will you know what to say? Have you taken your "inherited faith" and built upon it? Have you turned it into a relationship with Christ that is all your own? Is it a reasonable faith or just accepted dogma? Some of us approach our faith much like the fearful servant in the Parable of the Talents. We take what little we have been given and bury it, never seeking to grow it into some thing more, certainly not a faith that would lead Christ to say, "Well done, good and faithful servant. You have been faithful over a few things; I will set you over many things. Enter into the joy of your lord."

Sadly, for many people, their religion is largely a matter of proximity. Noted author and atheist, Bertrand Russell, said this:

> "...people choose the book considered sacred by the community in which they are born, and out of that book they choose the parts they like, ignoring the rest."

It is hard to argue against that point. Do we really choose our faith or is it largely chosen for us by our parents and the culture into which we happen to be born? Of course, how we arrive at our faith in Christ does not affect the objective truth of it. However, most Christians in the Western World, especially those of us in the United States, live in a state that approaches blasphemy. We live a life in which we acknowledge that there is a God but deny Him the attributes that He possesses or add to Him those that He condemns by believing in aspects of other religions or New Age spirituality simply because we are ignorant of our own professed beliefs.

Or, we simply relegate our faith to an afterthought in our lives, placing it somewhere after work, family, and perhaps even hobbies. Sadly, we live in a self-perpetuating cycle wherein we are handed a faith that is nothing more than a cultural or family institution. We then take this set of beliefs for granted and are content to go through the motions, never aspiring to a real relationship with Christ or with our fellow believers. We are sleepwalking towards eternity, being lulled by a

10

complacent institutional Christianity rather than seeking an active, vibrant one-on-one relationship with Jesus Christ. Many of us do not know what it is that we profess to believe or why we should believe it. We don't understand the importance of things like prayer or Bible study or praise and why these things are more than routine obligations but are holy acts of communion that connect every aspect of our being with our Eternal Father. And, failing this relationship, its no wonder that so many of us relegate our entire spiritual existence to, at best, one Sunday morning per week, for a single service that simply cannot be enough to teach us, inspire us, or feed the soul's innate longing for Christ.

Our faith doesn't even rise to the level of the cynical pragmatism of Pascal's Wager. No matter how misguided and fruitless that approach may be, its still requires a level of thought and consideration that many of us never bother to put into our Christian walk. One has to wonder how many people, self-proclaimed Christians, many of whom we see in church with us every week, never really even made a conscious choice to accept Jesus Christ as their personal savior. How many people inherited their faith, have maintained it, and adhere to it publicly, but have never actually asked Jesus to be lord of their lives? How many of us are unwittingly destined to hear Christ tell us, "I never knew you; depart from Me." It may seem like I am arguing semantics, but there is a huge gulf between stating, "I am a Christian" and declaring "I am a follower of Jesus Christ!"

11

Our cities, our nation, the whole world is devolving into chaos and the societies that claim to be "Christian" are in large part leading the way. The simple fact is this: an institutional faith that just seeks to "get by" will not save us any more than it glorifies God. As Christians we need to engage both our hearts and our minds to grow in our relationship with Christ in order for the "good infection" to spread from into us into society. The key to real change lay in the hands of the church and the strength of its relationship to Christ. As God said to King Solomon:

> If I shut up heaven that there be no rain, or if I command the locusts to devour the land, or if I send pestilence among my people; If my people, which are called by my name, shall humble themselves, and pray, and seek my face, and turn from their wicked ways; then will I hear from heaven, and will forgive their sin, and will heal their land. Now mine eyes shall be open, and mine ears attent unto the prayer that is made in this place. For now have I chosen and sanctified this house, that my name may be there for ever: and mine eyes and mine heart shall be there perpetually.

However, actually knowing why you believe what it is that you believe is a tall order. The Bible, after all, is not a book for those who lack a serious mind: those who would mistakenly decry its worth because it advocates slavery, spousal subservience, is anti-science, and the like. Sure, Christians down through the ages have been guilty of these things and much worse, but it is despite, not because of the Scriptures.

Nor is the Bible a book that we should take lightly, the way one would read a bit of fluff like a romance novel or a comic book. Again, it takes a serious mind and diligence. Therefore, my goal, albeit in a very small way, is to ask people to engage their minds with some of the basic questions. Why we believe what we believe. How should we act? What is our role in the body of Christ? That said, these may not be your basic questions and, even if they are your questions, these may not be the same answers at which you arrive. That is of no concern. This was my journey and everyone travels his or her own path to the cross. But, if we can all meet on the common ground of John 14:6, "Jesus saith unto him, I am the way, the truth, and the life: no man cometh unto the Father, but by me," the rest will work its way out. And, in the end, if this does nothing more than to cause someone to turn to the scriptures in order to fact check me or prove me wrong on some point, then I will consider this a success!

Ultimately we have four inescapable duties that we must attend to; four duties that serve as the pillars of our faith, upon which everything is built. We must believe with all our hearts. We must learn to the fullest capabilities that God has given each one of us. We must live a life that pleases God and accurately represents Him to the rest of the world. Moreover, we must love; not the love of romantic comedies and bad literature, but the love that is inherent in our Heavenly Father and we share through Him.

A Well Spent Misspent Youth

First, let me offer up a little background on myself. I was one of those who I spoke of earlier. I was born into my faith by virtue of Christian parents. And I grew to hate it. I think I hated getting up on Sunday mornings to go to church more than I hated getting up Monday through Friday to go to school. At least at school there was recess. There was the playground, friends and studies, which I found oddly interesting. I have always been something of a geek in that regard. But, with church, you sat there and sang boring, old songs. Or you sat there and listened to the preacher drone on and on... Or, you went to Sunday school or kids' church and sat there, listening to a more age appropriate drone from the pastor's wife. Not the sort of thing that made me want to get out of bed early on a weekend morning. I just did not get why I should be there and not somewhere else. My heart and my mind were somewhere else, why not my body, too?

But, on the other hand, many things from that time hold a special place in my memory even today, some 30+ years later. I still remember going to the pastor's house for Sunday lunches and once even for a Tupperware party. I remember the uncomfortable pews, the damp and somewhat creepy basement that housed the Sunday school classrooms, and the sonorous booming voice of "Old Man" Hibbard whose bass filled the building as he provided a "call and response" for "Have a Little Talk with Jesus."

I also remember one church program in particular where I had to go in front of everybody and recite a verse from memory. I was not then, nor am I now, the sort of person who relishes the limelight. I do not like public speaking and I certainly do not care to perform. Nevertheless, after many hours of practice, I committed my verse to memory and stood upon the small stage along with the other children. When it was my turn, I took the microphone and said:

> *John 3:16 for God so loved the world, He gave His only begotten son, that whosoever believeth in Him shall not perish, but has everlasting life.*

I took my place back in line, my heart slowly returning to its normal rhythm, while the next kid took his turn. I have lived in the same house now for about 8 years; I can't remember when trash pick-up day is for our neighborhood. I sometimes forget my kids' birthdays. I'm not entirely sure about what happened between the moments I awoke this morning until now! However, I have always remembered John 3:16. Throughout my rebellious high school years when I would fake a sickness so I wouldn't have to go to church (hmmm sick every Sunday morning, I wonder if my parents ever caught on!), to my college years when I proudly proclaimed that I was an atheist, a man of reason, John 3:16 could always be recalled from the depths of my memory as if that church program had just happened yesterday. In some ways, it was just one of the left behind memories of my youth; bicycles, baseball cards and church programs featuring some reluctant young boy that vaguely resembles the man I am today. In other ways, it was an anticipation of the things to come. In retrospect, that promise has been a beacon shining in the night, no matter how far away from the shore I let myself be pulled, that has shone as bright as ever: a warm welcoming glow of love, of faith, and of life everlasting.

The New Northern Kingdom

DMV Christians

And the Lord said to Hosea, Go, take upon thee a wife of whoredoms and children of whoredoms: for the land hath committed great whoredom, departing from the Lord – Hosea 1:2

It is a sad irony that the United States, a nation that has the greatest percentage of self-professing Christians of any nation in the world, may also be one of the most morally hollow nations, as well. According to a Pew Poll on Religion and Public Life, over 75% of Americans call themselves a Christian of some denomination. Yet, only 56% say their religion is an important aspect of their lives. Let that inconsistency sink in for a moment. Large portions of people who call themselves Christians do not consider their faith to be an important aspect of their lives.

I disagree with the conclusions reached by atheists, but I see their logic. I can track their thought pattern from point A to point B. But, this statistic leaves me dumbfounded. Its one thing to deny the existence of a Supreme Being and live a materialistic life based upon the now, upon satisfying only your own needs or tending to the worldly needs of your loved ones. That behavior is consistent with one's belief system. However, to profess a belief in God, as 75% of us claim to, but to relegate Him to an afterthought, a secondary concern, is borderline blasphemy.

I think the inconsistency is accounted for by another statistic. In that same study, it was found that only 39% of us regularly attend a church service. The sad fact is that most of us depend upon the church service for nearly, if not all, of our time spent with God. Praise, prayer, study, community with fellow believers, all of the vital aspects of our spiritual life, are too often confined to one building, on one morning, once a week. Therefore, it should come as no surprise that, with church attendance so low, that many of us consider our faith less important than our job, our friends and family, even our hobbies.

Many of us approach church in the same manner in which our children approach school: doing the bare minimum possible and complaining about any homework. And so, if we enter into God's presence only once a week, it is no wonder that so many of us don't consider our faith to be an important part of our lives. It is not a relationship; it is a weekly appointment.

So, why the incongruity between whom we say we are and the faith we claim to have? Simple, our "Christianity" is, to a great degree, more of a social construct than it is a personal relationship. It is the institution bequeathed to us by our parents; a responsibility to maintain and upkeep rather than a faith and relationship that we strive to cultivate. As such, for many of us, our approach to our spiritual life has more in common with standing in line at the Department of Motor Vehicles to renew our driver's license than it does with a growing and intensifying lifelong love affair with Jesus Christ.

I don't like going to the DMV and I sure don't want a DMV church. No one who calls himself or herself a Christian should settle for that.

You Are Not My People…

As Americans, we find ourselves very much in the same position that the prophet Hosea encountered when God directed him to speak out against the Northern Kingdom of Israel. After the death of King Solomon, Israel divided into two separate nations: the Southern Kingdom, also as known as Judah, under Solomon's son, Rehoboam; and the Northern Kingdom, known as Israel. The tribes of the north had refused to accept Rehoboam as the rightful successor to the throne and seceded from the kingdom.

After sixty years of war between the two kingdoms, there was an alliance established that largely ended the hostilities. Israel enjoyed a time of relative peace and prosperity. However, unlike Judah in the south, their actions showed that they had turned away from the God they had previously professed to follow. The Northern Kingdom turned to idolatry; they became a nation of violence, political disputes, arrogance, and ingratitude. They were also financially and militarily dependent upon other nations in order to maintain their safety and standard of living. A disarmament treaty with Damascus greatly limited their ability to field an army and their tribute payments to Assyria ate away at the nation's wealth.

God, through Hosea, called Israel to repent. Hosea married a prostitute to symbolize how Israel had become an unfaithful bride. God's words to Israel should be a wake up call to the 44% of Americans who claim to be Christian but also fail to consider their faith an important part of their lives:

> *Hear the word of the Lord, ye children of Israel: for the Lord hath a controversy with the inhabitants of the land, because there is no truth, nor mercy, nor knowledge of God in the land. By swearing, and lying, and killing, and committing adultery, they break out and blood toucheth blood. Therefore shall the land mourn, and every one that dwelleth therein shall languish with the beasts of the field…*

Perhaps those words should be a wake up call to every one of us. Those words could easily be spoken to the United States of America, right now.

Once Israel had turned away from God and turned to idolatry and to their own selfish desires, the Lord spoke through Hosea by the naming of one of his sons: "Then said God, call his name Loammi: for ye are not my people, and I will not be your God." What frightening words to hear from our Lord. However, those words fell upon deaf ears. The result was the end of the nation of Israel. God used the armies of Assyria to pass judgment and the Northern Kingdom disappeared into the dust of history. About a century later, the Babylonians would conquer the people of the Southern Kingdom; however, they would maintain their identity and their faith and would be reinstated into their homeland. The people of the Northern Kingdom were scattered throughout the lands of the conquering Assyrian empire, their history, their culture, their way of life were simply no more. They were wiped off the face of the earth for having turned their backs on God, embracing idolatry and living a life of sin and violence.

But we're the United States. That can't happen to us; we're a "Christian" nation! In reality, we are not so different from the people of Israel.

Sadly, in America the divorce r a t e among self-professed Christians is not markedly less than it is among non-Christians. Consider the terrible irony that the covenant of marriage, the human relationship that

21

symbolizes Christ's relationship with His church, is just as fragile amongst His own people as it is among those who deny Him. Perhaps our infidelity to each other stems from our infidelity to the Bridegroom. If we cannot be faithful to Christ, what is the likelihood that we will ever be able to be faithful to each other? If anything, divorce seems to be the common denominator across all faiths in the United States. Protestant, Catholic, evangelical, non-evangelical and atheist or agnostic; the statistics are virtually identical. If there were a Scriptural bias against divorce, one would never know it by looking at actions of the church. The stigma of divorce, whether it is social or religious, has all but vanished. And, as marriage has been de-valued, the family (the building block of society) has gone with it. The foundation of civilization is being dismantled and the church is assisting in its demolition.

Roughly the same percentage of young, unmarried Christians who believe that pre-marital sex is morally wrong (76%), still choose to do it with few stopping at just one partner and many, more than 25%, involving an abortion. Increasingly, children born to unwed parents are the norm.

The Old Testament tells of a certain pagan god that many peoples throughout the region worshipped: the god Moloch. The Ammonites, the Canaanites, Phoenicians, even as far away as Carthage, practiced the worship of Moloch. Moloch even finds his way into John Milton's *Paradise Lost* and Allen Ginsberg's "Howl." Throughout the Old Testament, Jehovah expressly forbids the worship of Moloch, under the punishment of death. The worship of this pagan god is one of the practices in Israel that brought God's Judgment upon them. Why such a strong reaction to this one of many competing regional deities? One reason was that the adherents of Moloch regularly practiced child sacrifice. The 12th century rabbi, Rashi, describes their ritual:

> *Moloch, which was made of brass; and they heated him from his lower parts; and his hands being stretched out, and made hot, they put the child between his hands, and it was burnt; when it vehemently cried out; but the priests beat a drum, that the father might not hear the voice of his son, and his heart might not be moved.*

The most common reason to sacrifice one's child to Moloch was in hopes that the pagan deity would bless the family with prosperity. In the hopes of financial gain, families would murder their own newborns. Thank God, we are so much more civilized than they…

Over 1 million (1,000,000) abortions are performed every year in the United States. Forty percent of minors who have had an abortion claim that their parents never even knew. It is estimated that, at current rates, nearly 1/3 of all American women will eventually have an abortion. Since the Supreme Court legalized abortion in Roe v Wade, there have been over 50 million abortions performed in the United States. That is more than the entire population of Spain and roughly the combined population of California and New York. What is the most common reason for having an abortion: money or, to be more precise, the lack of it. We will go into debt, take on a second job, beg, borrow, and steal to be able to afford a new car, a vacation, more high-tech toys, but a child is expendable.   Fifty million children, sacrificed to Moloch, the 21st century pagan God of Choice.

In Paradise Lost, Milton describes Moloch as one of the fallen angels, a demon-warrior:

> *MOLOCH, horrid King besmear'd with blood*
> *Of human sacrifice, and parents tears,*
> *Though, for the noyse of Drums and Timbrels loud,*
> *Their children's cries unheard that passed through fire*
> *To his grim Idol*

Thank God, we are so much more civilized than they…

At least half of us, including a majority of laypeople in the Catholic Church, support gay marriage and are open to homosexual couples adopting children.   Two decades ago, homosexuality couldn't even be mentioned in polite conversation now it provides the premise for sit-coms and parades down Main Street.   In no issue in contemporary America, do we find a better example of the deification of the Self, the usurpation of God's authority, than that of homosexuality. Paul says as much in Romans 1:24-27

> *Therefore God gave them over in the desires of their hearts to impurity, to dishonor their bodies among themselves.   They exchanged the truth of God for a lie and worshiped and served the creation rather than the Creator, who is blessed*

forever! Amen. For this reason, God gave them over to dishonorable passions. For their women exchanged the natural sexual relations for unnatural ones, and likewise the men also abandoned natural relations with women and were inflamed in their passions for one another. Men committed shameless acts with men and received in themselves the due penalty for their error

With homosexuality, we see God's abandonment of the unrepentant sinner. We all sin, but few of us approach our sins like those who practice homosexuality. Could you ever imagine adulterers, liars, thieves, etc…asking for tolerance, for acceptance of their sinful acts? Would they ever ask for legal protections for their "right" to commit adultery, to steal? With homosexuality, you see the worst perversion of one of the greatest attributes of God: love. The acceptance of homosexuality by the church is the starkest and yet most subtle blasphemies of our age: the substitution of Godless love in place of the love of God.

The line that separates acceptable from unacceptable behavior is constantly being pushed further away from Biblical truths, all in the name of a manmade perversion of the love of God; and the further it moves out, the less likely we will ever be able to pull it back. We are simply inviting the abandonment wrath of God.

We are a nation of professed "Christians" and yet, at the same time, we are a nation of criminals and potential victims. Consider these FBI statistics for 2009:

Murders – 15,000

Rapes - 89,000

Aggravated Assaults – 800,000

Burglaries -- 2.2 million

Vehicle thefts – 800,000

Larceny-Thefts – 6 million

Do you suppose that the list of the 75% who claim to be Christians and the list of people committing the crimes mentioned above overlap at any point? Maybe that's why church attendance is so low; people are too busy committing crimes!

In a nation that is 75 "Christian":

5 out of 100,000 of us are murdered

30 out of 100,000 of us are raped

260 out of 100,000 of us are assaulted

3000 out of 100,000 of us have our property stolen

A quote often attributed to Billy Graham, but actually said by his wife Ruth, sums up the current spiritual climate in the United States very succinctly:

"...if God doesn't come soon and bring judgment upon the United States, He's going to have to apologize to Sodom and Gomorrah!"

Pagan America

In fact, the United States may be much closer to being a pagan nation, as opposed to a Christian nation, than many people realize. In his book *Futurecast,* researcher George Barna tracked religious trends among Americans from 1991 to 2011. One of his chief findings is that the United States is quickly becoming a nation of "310 million people with 310 million religions…We are a designer society. We want everything customized to our personal needs — our clothing, our food, our education" and now our religion. More people are saying that they believe in "god" and may even accept Jesus Christ and believe that they are going to Heaven, but from there things get a little convoluted. Fewer and fewer people are going to church and only 7% believe in the in seven essential doctrines as defined by the National Association of Evangelicals' Statement of Faith. "Controversial" things like:

> 1) We believe the Bible to be the inspired, the only infallible, authoritative Word of God.

> 2) We believe that there is one God, eternally existent in three persons: Father, Son and Holy Spirit.

> 3) We believe in the deity of our Lord Jesus Christ, in His virgin birth, in His sinless life, in His miracles, in His vicarious and atoning death through His shed blood, in His bodily resurrection,

in His ascension to the right hand of the Father, and in His personal return in power and glory.

4) We believe that for the salvation of lost and sinful people, regeneration by the Holy Spirit is essential.

5) We believe in the present ministry of the Holy Spirit by whose indwelling the Christian is enabled to live a godly life.

6) We believe in the resurrection of both the saved and the lost; they that are saved unto the resurrection of life and they that are lost unto the resurrection of damnation.

7) We believe in the spiritual unity of believers in our Lord Jesus Christ.

What has emerged is a "Christian influenced" buffet approach to spirituality in which the person's needs are paramount and they pick and choose from the various beliefs systems what ever it is that suits them at the moment. If anything, what we have is an amalgamation of the post-modern suspicion of objective truth that seeks to de-mystify Jesus by reducing him to the level of just another moral teacher, but at the same time promotes other types of personal mysticism, individualized paths to some self-defined salvation. America is less of a Christian nation and more of an "emergent church" nation with the emphasis not on Christ as Christ, per se, but on Christ as one of many examples of how to live. As such, He could easily be replaced by Gandhi or Martin Luther King or even Che Guevara in many people's minds and they wouldn't miss a beat. Over 500 years after the Copernican Revolution, we have succeeded in putting Man back at the center of the universe but have left very little room for the Creator.

It's hard to say which came first: the institutional Christian or the institutional church, but they feed off each other. Our nation is defined by the *a la carte Christian* who seeks comfort and affirmation and by the institutional pastorate that gives it to them in a doctrine-lite message meant to offend as few as possible. By prosperity preachers whose message is that a good life is one of material success and that the size of one's bank account is a reflection of your closeness to God; pastors who are afraid to stand up for the Word out of fear of offending their "mega-congregations" and thereby reducing their own "closeness to God," aka their cash flow. We have diminished and marginalized God and His principles in order to create a belief system that is about us, that is driven by daytime talk show hosts who peddle books by the latest guru and who pad their bank accounts by adding leaven to our already bloated sense of self-worth.

We are too seeker friendly and not Christ-centered nearly enough. We have more pastors concerned about winning congregants for themselves than we have those who are driven by a passion to bring people to God. Rather than being a corporate body that takes the Word to society, we are a society of individuals that infuses our own priorities into our religion. In doing so, we create a

God based around ourselves; a protean deity that surrenders the truth to us only after it takes on our shape.

Like the people of Ninevah upon hearing the warnings of the reluctant prophet, Jonah, can we put a stop to our own destruction? What would it take? Simply put, it takes the people of God turning to Him. We can rail against politicians all we like, we can hold crooked businessmen up to scorn to our hearts' content, we can point the finger of shame at non-Christians until our whited sepulchres shine brilliantly in the sun, and we are only assuring our own downfall. Scripture tells us very clearly how to heal our land. God's people, who are called by His name, are to humble ourselves, and pray, and seek His face, and turn from our wicked ways; then He will hear from heaven, and will forgive our sins, and heal our land. But, can we do that as Institutional Christians, as DMV Christians? Can we truly do that if we don't even know why or what we believe in the first place? Will we also be destroyed for a lack of knowledge?

Time is short. There is much to learn because there is much to share!

Believe - There is a God

Why Do You Believe?

Job 19:25 For I know that my redeemer liveth, and that he shall stand at the latter day upon the earth.

If you take the average Christian and ask them why they believe in God, you are likely to get a blank stare or, if you do get an answer, it will probably be a rambling spiel about how they just "feel" it to be true or that it is just the way they were raised. The truth is that most Christians in the Western world are Christians because the West is Christian. If these same people had been born in Riyadh, they would probably be using the same justification for believing in the inerrancy of Mohammed. If they had been born in New Delhi they would probably "feel" the same certainty about their sacred cow. The truth is that most

31

Christians don't know why they are Christians outside of the fact that that is the culture into which they were born. We were simply born Christians in the same way that we are born Americans, or Texans, or New Yorkers.

If we truly believe that our faith in Christ is the objective truth, would we have been able to find our way to that truth had we not been born in a predominately Christian society? If your luck had been different and you had been born in Saudi Arabia, to a Muslim family, believing now that the only path to salvation is through Jesus Christ, do you believe that your examination of your own beliefs is rigorous enough to be able to discern the truth from as far away as Riyadh or would you still be just one of a billion Muslims? Is your salvation a by-product of chance, of good luck?

Does this seem like a pointless intellectual exercise? It shouldn't. Our culture, the character of our society is shaped by the actions of every one of us, more precisely, by the majority of us. Are we, as Christians, creating a society in which Jesus matters? Do we exemplify that to those around us? Or, are we typifying the attitude that Jesus is just one of many options by treating our relationship with Him as an afterthought?

If the Christian's Great Commission is to take the redemptive promise of Christ to an unbelieving world, how effective can we be if we don't know why we believe what we believe? If an atheist, or a Muslim, or a Hindu or a Scientologist comes to you and says, "Why should I believe as you believe," what will you say? Now, I realize that Christ tells us in Matthew:

> But when they deliver you up, take no thought how or what you shall speak: for it shall be given you in that same hour what you shall speak. For it is not you that speak, but the Spirit of your Father which speaks in you.

Moreover, I firmly believe this to be true. However, I also know that we are not meant to be benchwarmers, sitting listlessly on the sidelines, waiting for the Spirit to call our number. We need to dedicate ourselves to knowing what it is that we believe, like the Bereans. In the book of Acts, Luke tells us of the people of Berea who received the Word with a ready mind but also searched the Scriptures daily to prove whether the things they were being told were true.

A devotion to getting into the Word of God on a daily basis, along with a healthy prayer life, is one of the most important and fruitful steps that any Christian will ever take. Consider this admonishment from Proverbs:

> 4:07 Wisdom is the principal thing; therefore get wisdom: and with all thy getting get understanding.

Scripture is the source of that wisdom. It doesn't take a genius to understand the Bible; it just takes the Holy Spirit.

I was a Christian because my parents were Christians and I never knew anything different. We lived in a small town in Oklahoma where there were more varieties of Baptist churches than there were gas stations. If it were to be broken down, there was probably a church for every 50 people in town, which is amazing considering that the average Sunday morning crowd was probably less than 20 people.

So, I was taken to church at birth and I stayed in church until I learned, probably from my older brothers, various ways of getting out of it, such as the aforementioned "Sunday Morning Flu". Eventually my parents gave up even asking me to go with them. They knew there would be a litany of excuses as to why I couldn't go and I wouldn't accept any reasons as to why I should go. Oh, I still believed in God, I just couldn't be bothered with Him. My time was just too valuable.

So, I floated through the last few years of high school as what my mom would refer to as a backslider. I was worried about cars (not having one), girlfriends (not having one), and trying to earn enough money to afford those things. God was as absent from my mind as a black hole in the furthest reaches of the universe. Sure, if pressed, I would acknowledge that there was such a thing, however, I had seen it and it really didn't matter all that much too me.

Then, I went to college…

That was my Great Awakening or, more appropriately, the beginning of The Great Slumber. No one had ever told me there were so many different ways to look at the world. And, get this, they're all equally valid! There really is no "right" or "wrong," there are only differences in opinion. They never told me that at Konawa High School. Granted, terms like moral relativism and names like Friedrich Nietzsche weren't part of the secondary school curriculum, but somebody could have at least dropped a hint in my direction. This moral relativism thing would have been great ammunition when I got into an argument with my parents. How can you ground someone in the absence of an objective standard of right and wrong? Seriously! A ten o'clock curfew may have fit perfectly into their value system but I felt that it was immoral to be home any earlier than midnight!

So, my mind, which I had long ago emptied of anything other than football stats and Led Zeppelin trivia, was a ripe target for the professors and their brand of secular humanism. To be fair, I did have professors who were men and women of faith, but unlike the atheists, they kept their personal beliefs largely to themselves. Besides, to an eighteen year old who had barely even been out of the state of Oklahoma, the atheist, Marxist, gay teacher who cussed like a sailor with the zeal of a Pentecostal preacher at a tent revival was just more exciting! It's almost as if I was "entertained" out of my faith. Who knows, had the Christian teachers put on a better show, maybe I would have gone the other direction. But, my own beliefs were so shallow and so fragile that they were up for bid to whoever had the best one-liner.

Very soon, I was off and running: a Man of Reason. You want to convince me? Show me empirical evidence. If it cannot be measured through one of the five senses, it cannot exist. I was captivated by John Locke's "tabula rasa" idea that we are born blank slates upon which experience writes. Moreover, as a burgeoning libertarian, I even forgave Locke's Christian faith in view of his contribution to limited government by way of his Second Treatise on Civil Government. Then, oh boy, I found Ayn Rand! Talk about the whole package. Rationalistic, atheistic, libertarian (though she would never call herself that), and the ability to rhetorically shred every argument that crossed her path, at least I thought so. God was dead and in His place was the "New Joe," the Übermensch. This pretty much all happened by my second year.

So, I was an atheist. Well, in retrospect, I probably just used atheism as an excuse. It was an intellectual facade to hide the fact that I was a lazy Christian. It was just easier to label myself an unbeliever than it was to explain why I was simply disregarding the being that created the universe and everything in it, including me. Rather than face up to the fact that I was a spiritual slob and unable to articulate, let alone, defend my beliefs, I just denied it all. I was like an ostrich with its head in the sand. It didn't make God go away, but it did afford me a vacation from reality. Besides, I was in college, surrounded by professors who mocked people of faith and shouted down any argument from faith as being asinine and not worthy of a "scholar". Belief in God was deemed antithetical to reason and, therefore, had no place in the classroom. So, I and many of my fellow travelers either bottled up our faith or denied it altogether, became "practicing atheists".   I threw off the bonds of an ancient belief system and gladly accepted the bonds of new one, secular humanism. I even read Sartre! I would announce to my friends, and anyone else who would listen, that I was an atheist, a warrior who had just overthrown the tyrannical king of Faith and installed Reason on the throne.

But, in many ways, it was thinkers like Rand and her uber-rational kindred that helped me find my way back to faith. They raised questions that could not be answered in a universe devoid of God. Philosophy took me around in circles and ultimately to a dead end and science was a lot like reading a description of a beautiful painting. It can tell you a lot about the painting, but it falls well short of experiencing it in person.

Throughout my time as an atheist there were always two questions that continued to lead me to doubt my doubt. First, no matter how much my professors tried to beat it out of my head; I could not get passed the idea that there was a universal idea of right and wrong. They would always point out the different societies and cultures which had value systems that accepted behavior radically different than ours, so different that we condemned it (i.e. child sacrifice, polygamy, cannibalism, etc...) and this was proof that values are relative, but what they failed to explain is why those cultures are so rare and why the overwhelming number of the rest of us unanimously condemn such behavior. It's not so much that values are relative but that some people deviate from the universal Right. I first encountered this idea in C.S. Lewis' Mere Christianity and it stuck. No other explanation that I have encountered explains our universal appeal to what seems like the same moral authority.

The second problem that stuck in my brain was my brain itself! Some simple form of life creeping out of the primordial ooze and then, over billions of years, evolving into a more complex form of life seemed logical. What I could never accept, however, was how this primal goo could ultimately manifest itself in the thinking, creative, emotional, morally driven creature that is Man. If, by some random event, inanimate material becomes animate material, and life in the form of mere electrical impulse emerges and begins the arduous trek up the Darwinian hill to complexity, where along the way did the physical mass that is the brain begin to incorporate these ethereal qualities of the mind?

These questions alone did not turn the tide, but they got me to thinking: if we all came to the same conclusion on morality, perhaps it is because there was an objective standard that somehow has been imprinted in us. Moreover, if the physical brain could also develop into a mind that was capable of things like creativity and love, perhaps it was designed this way according to the image of another.

Then there was the book of Genesis and that cosmic mustard seed...

Big Bang: The Universe in a Mustard Seed

...At the briefest instant following creation all the matter of the universe was concentrated in a very small place, no larger than a grain of mustard. The matter at this time was very thin, so intangible, that it did not have real substance. It did have, however, a potential to gain substance and form and to become tangible matter. - Nahmanides, 12th century Jewish scholar.

For me the jump from doubt to deism was accomplished largely with the help of a Belgian priest. It also helped that my college biology teacher was a Christian who was open about his faith. That was the first time that I had come across such a creature on campus: a man of faith AND science!

With what we know about the natural world, the origin of the universe and the nature of life itself, the evidence of some form of an animating force that exists outside of our limited view of existence seems self-evident. I know, the scientific community is still heavily skewed to disbelieve in a creator, but we must remember that these scientists were reared in the same academia t h a t attributes all expressions of faith to the simpleminded and uneducated. However, an honest appraisal of the evidence will at least break evenly between the two propositions of materialism and faith.

Take the origin of the universe, for example. At one time, the prevailing view was that the universe had simply always existed; this was called the Steady-State theory. There was no need for a creator because nothing was ever created. It just simply was, always. This point of view goes all the way back to Aristotle and beyond. However, as technology advanced and we were able to peer further out into the vastness of space, it became clear that the universe had some sort of a beginning. Of course, the scientific community was slow to accept this, even when the evidence led them to the conclusion. Albert Einstein famously introduced a "fudge factor" into his General Theory of Relativity in order to gloss over the fact that his findings led to the conclusion of an expanding or contracting universe, not a steady one. His atheistic worldview was more important to him than acknowledging the truth when he found it. Einstein knew that the consequences of an expanding universe would require a universe with a definite beginning and that this played right into the hands of those who argued for a creator. His findings also went against the accepted wisdom of thousands of years. So, he falsified his own work in order to maintain the illusion of a godless universe. Later he would say that his fudging of the theory was the "biggest blunder" of his life. However, despite claims to the contrary, Einstein never came to accept the existence of a personal God.

As early as 1912, many scientists were noting that the universe seemed to be expanding. Then, Georges Lemaitre, the aforementioned Belgian priest, astronomer and professor of physics at the Catholic University of Louvain, applied Einstein's General Relativity to cosmology and proposed the hypothesis of the "primeval atom". Lemaitre showed that the universe was not steady, but is actually expanding at a great rate. Moreover, if the universe is expanding, one could logically conclude that, if you hit the rewind button and moved backwards in cosmological time, that you would arrive at a "creation-event". This moment, at which the universe would have been infinitely small, infinitely dense, and infinitely hot, was known as a singularity. This singularity would have been the universe in a mustard seed, so to speak. All the matter that exists in the universe was compacted into one tiny spec. What we do not know, however, is where this singularity came from and what outside force acted upon it to make it expand. Everything we think we know happens after the expansion, anything before that is mere speculation. In a statement that means so much more than he probably intended, physicist Stephen Hawking (an atheist like Einstein) commented that we could not know much about the nature of this singularity because science cannot grasp the infinite. So true!

However, what the Big Bang did not do was to do away with the need for a creator. Einstein was right that the implications of an expanding universe made the idea even more palatable for those who were willing to be honest about the implications of the theory. As Arno Penzias, Nobel Laureate in Physics put it:

> *The best data we have [concerning the Big Bang] are exactly what I would have predicted had I nothing to go on but the five books of Moses, the Psalms, and the Bible as a whole.*

As Christians, we need to remember that any scientific theory that explains the birth of the universe, or any natural phenomena for that matter, need not be viewed by the church as a challenge to God's existence. We must always remember that science is essentially the study of our natural world, e.g. matter and energy and how they interact. God isn't constrained by the natural world anymore than a painter is constrained by the canvas upon which he paints. No new scientific discovery pushes God out of the picture; it only gives us another little glimpse of His majesty. From the tiniest subatomic particle to the great explosion that formed the very universe, we see God's handiwork. Moreover, when science and faith contradict, we simply need to look at our premise, on both sides of the equation. There is no assumed right side or wrong side. The science could be faulty and, just as easily, our interpretation of scripture could be wrong. Just ask Copernicus and Galileo!

Prior to Copernicus, the generally accepted theory was of that of a geocentric universe, that the earth was at the center, unmoving, and everything else revolved around it. This was known as the Ptolemaic System after the astronomer Ptolemy. The Catholic Church was partial to the idea of a geo-centric universe because it put the earth, and Man, at the center of all of God's creation. The church referred to verses such as:

> *Ecclesiastes 1:5 the sun rises and the sun goes down, and hastens to the place where it rises.*
>
> *Habakkuk 3:11 The sun and moon stood still in their habitation at the light of thine arrows as they sped, at the flash of thy glittering spear.*
>
> *Joshua 10:12-13 Then spoke Joshua to the Lord in the day when the Lord gave the Amorites over to the men of Israel; and he said in the sight of Israel, "Sun, stand thou still at Gibeon, and thou Moon in the valley of Aijalon." And the sun stood still, and the moon stayed, until the nation took vengeance on their enemies. Is this not written in the Book of Jashar? The sun stayed in the midst of heaven, and did not hasten to go down for about a whole day.*
>
> *1 Chronicles 16:30 tremble before him, all earth; yea, the world stands firm, never to be moved.*

These, and similar verses, were evidence to the church that it was the sun that revolved around the earth, and not the other way around. And, given the influence of the church, it remained the accepted theory for nearly 1400 years, that is, until Copernicus.

When the Renaissance astronomer, Nicolaus Copernicus first proposed the idea that the Ptolemaic model was wrong in his *De Revolutionibus*, it engendered very little controversy from the church. There was actually great interest in it. In 1536, Cardinal Nikolaus von Schönberg, Archbishop of Capua, wrote to Copernicus from Rome:

> *Some years ago, word reached me concerning your proficiency, of which everybody constantly spoke. At that time, I began to have a very high regard for you... For I had learned that you had not merely mastered the discoveries of the ancient astronomers uncommonly well but had also formulated a new cosmology. In it you maintain that the earth moves; that the sun occupies the lowest and t h u s the central, place in the universe... Therefore with the utmost earnestness I entreat you, most learned sir, unless I inconvenience you, to communicate this discovery of yours to scholars, and at the earliest possible moment to send me your writings on the sphere of the universe together with the tables and whatever else you have that is relevant to this subject...*

Even Pope Clement VII expressed interest in the new theory. By 1616, however, political tides had changed and *De Revolutionibus was* all but banned by the Catholic

Church on the basis that the heliocentric model was "false and altogether opposed to Holy Scripture."

Undaunted, Italian astronomer Galileo Galilei, with the aid of his more advanced telescope, took up the defense of the Copernican Model. For this, he was tried and convicted of heresy and sentenced to house arrest for the rest of his life. In 2000, Pope John Paul II issued a formal apology to Galileo and others whom the Church had mistreated over the last two millennia.

Ultimately, this wasn't an issue of faith versus science. It was more an issue of hermeneutics, Biblical interpretation. Neither Copernicus nor Galileo were out to overturn scripture; they, like Augustine, saw the verses in question as more poetic than literal. On the other hand, perhaps the passages just showed terrestrial-bound man, as best he could, describing the cosmos without the aid of the equipment and knowledge we take for granted. Besides, the claim that the earth occupied the center of the solar system was a position of the church, of man, not Scripture. Science was correcting mankind, not conflicting with God.

These kinds of conflicts have created a schism between faith and science that need not exist. Moreover, it is largely our fault. As Christians we dismiss or are hostile to science at our own peril. Science, at its best, is a window into the mechanics of God's creation. Think of the lyrics to the hymn "How Great Thou Art":

O Lord my God,

When I in awesome wonder

Consider all

The works Thy Hand hath made,

I see the stars,

I hear the mighty thunder,

Thy pow'r throughout

The universe displayed;

Don't be afraid of scientific revolutions; they are simply God pulling back the veil a little more and allowing us a glimpse of "he who made the earth by his power, who established the world by his wisdom and by his understanding, stretched out the heavens."

The Dawkins Delusion

Of course, it must be noted that today we face some of the most strident attempts that the church has ever seen to relegate faith to the superstitious Middle Ages, all in the name of Science. The proponents of this "New Atheism" seek not to get along with faith, but to assault it, to systematically wipe it out. The movement is led by what has come to be known as the "Four Horseman": Richard Dawkins, Christopher Hitchens, Sam Harris, and Daniel Dennett. The mantra of the New Atheist is that "religion should not simply be tolerated but should be countered, criticized, and exposed by rational argument wherever its influence arises." Their ultimate goal is, as Sam Harris writes in his *Letters to a Christian Nation*, "to demolish the intellectual and moral pretentions of Christianity in its most committed forms." Theirs is not an objective of peaceful coexistence or détente.

However, upon reading these gentlemen's work, one cannot but help to get the feeling that their atheism, and their pure hatred of God, informs their science much more than their science informs their atheism. Take this straw man that Dawkins sets up in his book, *The God Delusion*:

> "*However statistically improbable the entity you seek to explain by invoking a designer, the designer himself has got to be at least as improbable.*"

In other words, since creationists think that life is too complex to have arisen randomly (as the Darwinian materialists claim), any creator would necessarily be at least as, if not more, complex than the life you seek to explain. According to Dawkins, any creator must contain at least as much information as what it creates and information is inversely correlated to probability. Therefore, any God that could create everything would be too complex to be probable.

No wonder Dawkins is an atheist. His "god" is too small to believe in.

Can we not infer that any eternal, omnipotent, omniscient being with the ability to create life might in fact be infinitely complex and that the low probability that Dawkins posits says nothing more than that this being is unique (there is but one God), thereby accepting both the creator's infinite complexity and Dawkins' almost null probability?   Dawkins n e v e r   c o n s i d e r s   t h a t possibility , again he begins with his atheism and works back from there.

Another of the Four Horsemen of the New Atheism movement, Sam Harris, wrote a book entitled *Letter to a Christian Nation* that is remarkable in its false assumptions about w h a t C h r i s t i a n s b e l i e v e .   It is r e l a t i v e l y easy to dispute unmade contentions. For example,   Harris believes that we Christians maintain that our faith is an "unrivaled source of human goodness."   He goes to great lengths to show that, in their actions, Christians are no better than non-Christians and that there are other faiths, Jainism, for example, which preaches what Harris considers to be a more moral message, based largely upon their belief in complete nonviolence.

To the first claim, the heart of Christianity is our reliance on Jesus for salvation.   And, yes, there is, or should be, a distinctness of character that shows that rebirth through Christ.   But, most Christians will tell you that if you spend your time looking for a "human goodness" you'll have as much luck as Diogenes in his search for an honest man. Our faith is not about human goodness, but the recognition of our depravity and our hopelessness in the absence of Christ.   Being a Christian, in and of it self, doesn't bestow goodness upon us. Should a C h r i s t i a n h a v e a c h a r a c t e r t h a t r e s e m b l e s Christ? Yes. That is the lifelong process of sanctification that is only completed with glorification. But, the trappings of human goodness, worldly morality, which is what concerns Harris much more than Judeo-Christian ethics, is a wholly separate issue than the objective truth of Christianity. Harris doesn't get that; this is apparent by the fact that he holds Jainism up as superior to Christianity due to its tenet of universal non-violence. Absolute pacifism is not a Christian ideal. Therefore, the fact that Jains may adhere to it better than Christians is irrelevant. It's simply another straw man for Harris to erect and knock down.

According to Harris, the Jains surpass the morality of the Bible with one sentence:

> "Do not injure, abuse, oppress, enslave, insult, torment, or kill any creature or living being"

I wonder if Harris is a vegetarian, which is what this passage would require? I wonder if Harris believes that no war, or any form of self-defense, is ever justified, which is again, what this Jain precept would logically necessitate. It's ironic how often atheists ridicule Christian ethics as unrealistic and outdated but point at something like this as morally superior. How is living as a lamb being led to slaughter, literally living on grass, and considering human life so valueless that it should not be defended, an improvement over the Sermon on the Mount?

It is in these ethical obfuscations that Harris really falls short. Consider this passage:

Everything about human experience suggests that love is more conducive to happiness than hate. This is an objective claim about the human mind, about the dynamics of social relations, and about the moral order of our world. It is clearly possible to say that someone like Hitler was wrong in moral terms without reference to scripture.

As a Christian, I can agree with that statement. What Harris fails to do, however, is to grasp the ramifications of his statement.

Everything about human experience suggests that love is more conducive to happiness than hate. Why is that? If I take pleasure in hate, be it in the form of racism, misogyny, ageism, and homophobia, whatever.... What grounds do you have to say that my hate is inferior to your love? How is it an objective, universal standard that love is superior to hate? Its one thing to say that love is the superior emotion; it is quite another thing to explain why it is so.

It's an objective claim about the human mind and how we relate to one another and the moral order of the world. Okay. How did this objective standard become imprinted in our mind in order to shape our relationships and our moral order? Again, why? Just because Harris says so, I guess.

It is clearly possible to say that someone like Hitler was wrong in moral terms without reference to scripture. Yes it is. Because the moral law is written in us, in Harris' brain and in the Apostle Paul's heart, as he writes in his Epistle to the Romans. The moral law is manifest in us, Harris and I both agree on this; he simply stops before he gets to its source. He stops at the DNA-level; our morality is biological, instinctive. That is tantamount to claiming that a computer program originated on a disc and not giving the programmer his just credit.

But, Harris will point out; atheists can be moral, too! Yes, they can. An atheist can help the needy as good, if not better, than a person of faith. They can give to charity in greater amounts; they can spend more of their time doing volunteer work. And, yes, Christians can do exceedingly bad things. The same moral law is written on all of our hearts and an atheists can adhere to it without understanding its source and a Christian can know its source and fail to live up to it. None of this changes the reality that the moral law comes from God and nothing that Harris or any of his cohorts point to counters this simple fact.

Ultimately, the best atheism can manage is to cherry pick and mimic Judeo-Christian ethics and attempt to slap a veneer of biological determinism on it.

Harris, et al. will also tell us that there is an inherent lack of logic in any holy book that, while claiming to offer prophetic statements, fails to make any that has any real relevance to us today. Why, they ask, does this omnipotent God not offer any prophecies about something like the internet, space travel or anything to which 21st

Century man can relate? And why not dish a cure for cancer, while He's at it? Fair enough. In order to appease the New Atheists, God should have written the Bible in such a way as to make it unintelligible to the 2000 years of people who came before us. The Bible, they feel, should have been geared largely towards the brief period that they themselves occupy. That's a little egotistical, isn't it! Let's say that God did include a specific prophecy about, oh, let's say smart phones. The average "Old New Atheist" reader from just a century ago would have had no understanding of it and consider it meaningless gobbledygook. The average reader, especially the "New New Atheist" reader, a century from now would be thoroughly unconvinced by a prophecy of already antiquated technology. "Why not," the New New Atheists from a century into the future, would complain, "include a prophecy about OUR time?" And so the skepticism would continue on, ad infinitum, because those of this mindset are already closed off to any sort of evidence, anyway.

And why stop at cancer, what about AIDs, diabetes, baldness, acne...? Why couldn't Ezekiel tell me how to grow a better lawn, get better gas mileage, how to get ahead at work? How much accurate information would be required to win them over? Would there ever be enough? No, when it comes down to it, the New Atheists aren't concerned with winning minds over with facts; it's more about browbeating the weak with incomplete science and ad hominem attacks.

51

Skeptics about the validity of the Bible do not seem to understand that it isn't meant to address the minutiae of life for every period that has followed. If it were to include something to convince every person from every time period, it would be so voluminous and weighty that it would be nearly impenetrable to the average reader. The Bible ultimately has one purpose: to direct us to Christ and to force the choice between a life in Him or death apart from Him.

Goldilocks and the Cosmic Zone

Another point of contention between the New Atheists and faith is the evolutionary argument of the Anthropic Principle. This principle, simply put, is that life exists on earth because earth is uniquely situated to allow for that life. For example, we are just the right distance from the sun, not to close, not too far (the Goldilocks Zone), we have abundant water, we are protected from space debris by the outer planets, our orbit around the sun is the perfect shape, etc...

Now, the Creationist would argue that none of the things that make this planet suitable for life could be due to chance. For all of these things to come together to sustain life, there must have been the guidance of a divine hand. On the other hand, Dawkins and other Darwinians argue that Creationist have their causality backwards. The cosmic balance that allows for life was not created for us; we evolved here due to the balance that naturally existed.

Life on earth is the product of pure chance and an amenable environment.

I have never felt that the Anthropic Principle was a good argument for Creationists to hang their hat on, but I do have one issue with Dawkins here. If the origin of life is as he describes it, why have we not seen other forms of life on other planets already? Sure, earth is uniquely suited to the kind of life that evolved here, but what prevents other varieties of life from evolving everywhere, life suited to that particular environment? Our life requires water and a certain type of atmosphere and a certain temperature range, but does that mean that ALL forms of life must have the same things to evolve? If Dawkins is right, why has life not evolved on and adapted to environments on all planets? Granted, I will give him the fact that we are shielded from comets and asteroids by Jupiter is beneficial, but Mercury and Venus are shielded, as well. Why has life uniquely suited for those planets not evolved, as well? Surely, our "Goldilocks Zone" is not the only one capable of sustaining any form of life. If Dawkins is right, there would almost have to be life on other planets, of some form, already known to us.

But, perhaps I, as Dawkins points out about people of faith, just haven't had my "consciousness raised, as biologists have, by natural selection..."

There is also the issue of "fine tuning." There are so many variables in the universe that, if they were off by the least bit, the universe would be radically different and wholly incapable of producing or sustaining life. A few examples:

1) The strong nuclear force constant: this is the force that binds protons and neutrons together to for the nucleus of an atom. If this force were any stronger, there would be no hydrogen so the atomic formation of the most life essential elements would be impossible. Any weaker there would be no elements heavier than hydrogen, again preventing life.

2) The gravitational force constant: This finely balanced attraction exists between objects with mass. If it were any larger and stars would be too hot and burn out rapidly, preventing life from forming. Too small and the stars would be too cool and many of the elements needed for life would be unable to form.

3) The expansion rate of the universe: any faster no galaxies would be able to form. Any slower, the universe would begin to collapse back in on itself.

4) The decay rate of protons: If it were any faster, it would release too much radiation, killing all life. If it were any slower, it would not allow enough matter in the universe to support life.

5) The velocity of light: if it were any faster, stars would be too luminous to support life. If it were any slower, stars would not be luminous enough to support life.

These are just a few of the many forces in the universe that are fine tuned to an "nth" degree in order to allow for the development of life in the universe. There are many, many others involving things like the distance between stars, the initial uniformity of radiation, the fine structure constant, white dwarf binaries, supernovae eruptions, mass of the neutrino and on and on.....Again, the secular scientist will fault our causality. Life is here because of these things, these things are not so because a Creator intended for life to be here.

As the evidence of a design piles up, Dawkins, Hawking, Hitchens, et al. are content to rest in the certainty of their own delusions and accuse creationists of a "God of the gaps" approach to science. There are unknowns, they claim, and we deists are too ready to plug God into the gaps in our knowledge. Even Dietrich Bonheoffer, the German theologian who was executed for his role in plotting against Adolph Hitler, feared that attempts to explain the unknown with God would result in His diminishment when the gaps were eventually filled in by new scientific discoveries. And, perhaps this is true, but it is due to the fallacy that scientific discoveries explain away God. Scientific discoveries no more diminish God than understanding aerodynamics makes man's trip to the moon less of an accomplishment. The rocket did not make itself, it didn't pilot itself, and it didn't provide its own reason for going to the moon. There was a plan and a designer behind it all the way. In fact, the New Atheists are committing a "reverse God of the Gaps" approach to science where they write God out of any picture that man's feeble knowledge begins to comprehend. They worship the creation and disregard the Creator.

Stephen Hawking said that "the greatest enemy of knowledge isn't ignorance; it's the illusion of knowledge." I propose that the New Atheists and their philosophical forebears and compatriots are a prima facia case for that contention. For, although reason cannot prove that there is a God, otherwise faith would be unneeded, reason, and the continuing accumulation of supporting evidence, does lend weight to the fact that our faith is reasonable.

In fact, when you consider the whole picture, the mounting evidence that points towards a creator, maybe Richard Dawkins' previous assumption of greater complexity breeding complexity is fallacious. Perhaps the reality is just the opposite. Thomas Aquinas believed that God was simple, with no composition. Perhaps part of the beauty of God is His simplicity; a spirit, after all, has no parts. Moreover, when faced with competing premises that are increasingly, at the minimum, equal, perhaps it behooves us to choose the one that makes the fewest new assumptions: that of a Creator. What better illustration of Occam's razor could exist?

Anti-Theist or Just Anti-Christian

Confusing the manmade institution of religion, that is marred by the frailties of mankind, with the nature of God, Hitchens, Dawkins, et al. are less concerned with the likelihood o f God e x i s t i n g than they are w i t h t h e inconsistent actions of His followers. As such, the "New Atheists" would be easier to take seriously, if they lived up to their billing of being "anti-theists". However, this is not the case at all. The large part of their breath and print is spent railing against Christianity. They aren't "anti-theists" as much as they just hate the followers of Christ. They claim that their Christian focus is due to the fact that they live in nominally Christian nations and have been reared by a Christian culture, but what does it say about their claims to be non-biased arbiters of truth if they forgo a world largely defined by its war against global jihad to concentrate on slick televangelists and small town charlatans? The fastest growing and most violent religion in the world is hardly mentioned while Anglicans and Baptists are painted as the sources of all evil. I guess, to the "New Atheists," the nuisance of a Jehovah's Witness knocking on one's door is to be feared and reviled more than jihad, shariah law, and dhimmitude.

Christopher Hitchens likes to point out that, although many terrors have been committed in the name of religion, none has been committed because of non-belief. This, to Hitchens, shows the moral superiority of atheism or, at least the moral bankruptcy of faith. However, it misses the point altogether. Man will always be inhumane to one another and the professed "why" is usually just a cover. The many wars of so-called Christian nations, Hitchens would have us believe, are due to our faith but the secularism of the communist world is just a coincidence and unrelated to their near century long drive to spread Marxism by any means possible. The Arab-Israeli conflict could be solved if Yahweh and Allah would just butt out, but the secularism of Stalin, Castro, Chavez, Mao, etc...is irrelevant when considering the tens of millions who have died under their officially God-less regimes.

Hitchens is half-right. Atheism is not to blame for the Gulags, The Great Leap Forward, the Killing Fields of the Khmer Rouge, or any of the many other atrocities associated with secular regimes. However, neither is faith to be blamed for the wars that Hitchens and the rest lay at its feet. The secular humanism of the socialists is just a tool; it is the cover for the idiocy of human nature that is so often driven by envy and often manifests itself in policies of forced redistributionism. However, religion is just as often a cover, or scapegoat. Human nature, e.g. greed, envy, racism, whatever; drives us to do "x", so we whitewash our baser instincts and selfish goals with terms like faith, social justice, patriotism, or any other more noble ideal to take the edge off the reality. Nevertheless, it would seem that the New Atheists are willing to give secular tyrants a pass because they arrive at their policies via "reason" rather than faith. That, somehow, lessens the stain of their victims' blood.

This brings us to another of the secularists' arguments

with God: the existence of evil. It has long been argued by skeptics that no good god would allow us to live in such an exceedingly bad world. Wars, plagues, famines, children born with terrible diseases only to suffer through a short life…any god who would allow this to be the norm is either cruel, incompetent or simply non-existent. So, is it a logical contradiction to believe in a wholly, good God who would allow evil to exist as part of His creation? I think not. In fact, the possibility of the existence of evil is a necessary corollary to the existence of unfettered free will. If man is free to choose, then the possibility for man to choose that which is not good, is necessary.

Arguments against the existence of God due to the evil we encounter daily is much like a child thinking that his parent no longer loves him because the parent disciplined him or, even more apt, a child thinking that a parent no longer loves him because the child failed to heed the parent's warning about running over uneven ground and, as a result, fell and injured himself.

The child may think that the parent should have been more adamant in his warning to him. It seems to me that God was clear in his warning to Adam and Eve about which tree not to eat from and scripture is clear about the wages of sin. Those of us who feel we have not been adequately warned are simply living in denial.

The child may also think that the parent should have stopped him from running in the first place, thus removing his ability to act according to his free will. What kind of relationship could there be between man and God if we were created as will-less automatons in order to protect us from our own bad choices? I cannot imagine that any atheist, when presented with a safe but strictly predetermined existence, would actually opt for such a thing.

Finally, the child may think that the parent should have leveled the ground out in the first place, given them a smooth path on which to run. Isn't this what God initially gave humanity? When Adam and Eve fell, they took all of creation with them. God could not allow the willful sins of the pair to be ameliorated by existence in a perfect, unblemished world. In addition, that one willful act of disobedience introduced sin and death into the world for all who would come after and into nature itself.

We get what we get because God gave us the freedom to fail and we fail! Some may think that it is an evil, cruel world, but that is a consequence of our freedom. It is mankind and our choices that make it so, not God. A world without evil would probably be a world without good, as well. Without the freedom to choose between good and evil, we would be, at best, soulless animals with no concept of morality at all, or we would be robots pre- programmed to act by God, with no input of our own. God seeks a relationship with us and, in order for that to happen we must have the freedom to choose. Sometimes we choose poorly.

We are told that all of creation groans for its own redemption, for the day when it too will shed the bonds of sin and return to its intended state. Until then life for all of creation will be, to steal a line from Thomas Hobbes, "short, nasty, and brutish". Again, such are the wages of sin and the cost of freedom.

Be Prepared

I take this little detour to the work of the "New Atheists" and their intellectual kin for two reasons. First, to show a little bit of the circuitous path that I took back to faith through the science lab and elsewhere and to look at some of the primary "proofs" of a materialistic universe and how they failed to woo me back to doubt. But, primarily I bring them up to show the sorts of forays into "reason" that atheists are using to try to counter faith. I am not a scientist. I make no claim to understanding much of what people like Dawkins study and write about, but I think that I can spot faulty logic when confronted with it and all believers should be equipped to do so, as well. As C.S., Lewis writes in *Mere Christianity*:

> *God is no fonder of intellectual slackers than of any other slackers. If you are thinking of becoming a Christian, I warn you, you are embarking on something which is going to take the whole of you, brains and all.*

Even if you could care less about things like the Big Bang, the Anthropic Principle and the like, there are many who do, some of whom may be held back from a relationship with Christ because of the doubt instilled in them by the arguments of people in the media like Dawkins and even people in their classrooms. We don't need PhD's but we should be able to counter a fallacious argument when we encounter it. It may help a fellow traveler on his or her way to salvation. Again, we don't need PhD's in the various disciplines, but we need to know how to answer the skeptic.

Memories of Things Yet Seen

However, for those of us who aren't steeped in physics and Big Bang cosmology, where might our faith come from? It may be that we are born with a predisposition to faith. Researchers at Oxford University did a three-year study of the nature of faith that spanned 20 countries. Their conclusion: faith is in our genes. More than being a learned behavior or part of a pattern of socialization, human beings are "hardwired" to believe that there is something beyond our natural world. Now, this "something" can take many different forms around the world, but there is something about us as a species that seeks the spiritual. As such, atheists are the aberration.

Mankind, across all cultures, always seeks to deify something: the weather, volcanoes, totems, ancestors, etc... Why is this?

Atheists will say that it is our feeble way of trying to explain the unexplainable. They say that early man feared thunder, so he created a "thunder god" and then tried to appease this manmade deity. Or gods were created by the powerful in society to enforce codes of conduct on the masses. Now, I do not believe that truth is determined simply by the number of adherents to a proposition, but it never ceases to amaze me that in world where the estimates of self-described atheists or "nonreligious" are somewhere between 2% to 12% of the total population, that its so easy for skeptics to dismiss the faithful as idiots. I would wager that the number of people who think the moon landing was faked or that the moon is made of cheese is somewhere in the same 2-12% range.

No, this innate belief is more than a manmade construct devised to control our actions or to explain away natural phenomenon. There seems to be a shared "experience" across all of creation that has left an indelible imprint upon who we are as a creature. I use the word "experience" carefully for it is not an empirically quantifiable experience, per se, but rather a shared sense of "the other". This may be the "numinous" of German theologian Rudolph Otto, the "wholly other" that evokes a sense of *mysterium fascinans* in all who are open to it. It is a fact that there is, among nearly all human beings, an idea that there is something that makes our existence purposeful. Perhaps, embedded deep down in our genetic make-up, there is the imprint of a maker, much as an artist signs his paintings, which says, "This is the product of my labor and I call it my own."

Mankind is geared to believe in a creator and to believe that the creator is still involved in our lives on some level and atheists are the one's swimming against the stream of truth. John Calvin also believed that we are made with a natural inclination to believe and it was our sin nature that blunted this predisposition towards God. I would also add willful ignorance to the list of things that can separate us from our Creator, an ignorance born of and magnified by pride. The atheists like to think they are independent thinkers and they, like the man who tore free of his bonds in Plato's "Parable of the Cave," are the ones to walk out of the darkness and into the light. However, in reality, they are fighting against the nature instilled in us all to turn towards our Creator. Locke's slate is not so blank, after all, but the doubters are doing there best to wipe away the truth and rewrite man's story with a secular god of their own making.

Our soul's natural inclination is towards God, to tear free of the earthly and temporal bonds of this life and to rejoice in the timeless presence of Him for whom it was created. Sadly, our soul and our will are often working towards different goals. While our souls desire divine union with the Everlasting, our will is often driven by desires of the moment, of the here and now. As the old hymn goes, this world is not our home; therefore, the battle that must be won is the earthly submission of the will, usually against its own desire, to God. Only once the will is placed in His hands, under His control, can the soul begin its blessed ascension. This is no easy battle; the will has many allies in this world: the weakness of the flesh, family and friends, the media, our own sinful nature, even time itself. However, the soul has the one great ally that it needs and that ally has a toehold in our will, if we will only acknowledge it. The fact that we are made in His image has left a part of our will predisposed to let the soul free to take wing, to open the door to the cage that the rest of our will pieces together, bar by bar. When Christ stands at the door and knocks, it is that part of the will, His holy imprint, which allows us to choose to answer the call.

All Roads Lead To Jesus

"Having fully realized that the whole world is dissolving before our very eyes, it is impossible to ask a more far-reaching question than this: 'Do you believe in Jesus Christ?' " - Dr. Charles Malik, past Secretary General of the UN

Even if one accepts that there is a cosmic conductor, why choose a Christian one? What is it about Christianity that makes it true while all other religions are false? For me, the existence of a Creator is of itself logical evidence for the validity of the Judeo-Christian narrative. Why? Because it is the only faith that has a Creator that seems to genuinely care for His creation. Nearly every civilization has had a creation myth of some stripe. The Sumerian creation story on the tablet of Nippur, the Cherokee Indians and the Water Beetle narrative, the Mayan gods creating man from the sacred maize, the Greeks began with the yawning void of Chaos that produced the early gods, and so on. However, what most world religions lack is a Creator that takes a genuine interest in humanity. Many of the other religions feature deities that run the gamut from ambivalence to hostility towards their creation; the Greeks having gods that are both. However, only the Judeo-Christian god takes the logical step of being interested in and caring about His handiwork. This makes sense. Why create all of this if you really do not care about it?

That is where I find the truth in Christianity that is lacking from other religions. The creator, a loving father, who treats his creation as sons and daughters, not pawns in a game, not enemies to malevolently thwart at every turn, but in the way that we would expect a parent to act towards his children. God is love, God is logical, and it is only logical that God would love his creation. It is for this reason, that only the Judeo-Christian narrative rings true. Therefore, my faith in Christ is simple, some would say simplistic. I love Him because He first loved me.

Moreover, what are we to make of the apostles, what of their actions after the death of Christ? If they truly saw Jesus die and entombed like any other false prophet, they must have had an incredible will to carry on the lie of Jesus as Messiah. Ask yourself, would you willingly die in order to perpetuate what you know to be a lie? Would you suffer torture, imprisonment, and a horrible death for no other reason but to continue a grand deception long after you no longer walked the earth? This is the question we have to ask about the original disciples of Jesus Christ. These men walked with Jesus, heard his teachings, and accepted him as the Messiah, the incarnate Son of God. Believing this to be true, they dedicated their lives, unto death, to preaching His gospel, even after seeing Christ's arrest, trial, torture, and execution. If the historical Jesus was but a man, who, after being taken down from the cross, was laid in the tomb of Joseph of Arimathea to slowly decompose just like any other living thing, why would the disciples bother carrying on with the lie? There was no money to be gained? No popularity, as their message made them hated, outcasts among their own people. Upon seeing their Christ's lifeless body, entombed, why did they continue to tell the world that Jesus was the Son of God, even at great risk to their own lives? Were they all lunatics? Were they simply obstinate to the end? Or did they really see their risen savior and that gave them the strength to spend the rest of their lives travelling the known world, in and out of prison, ostracized from their own people, and finally facing death in order that others may live in Him?

Consider the fates of these men (the original twelve and Paul) who Jesus called to be his disciples:

Peter, Simon Peter, Cephas, "the Rock," a fisherman picked by Jesus to be a follower and one of the most prominent of the disciples. He is also shown to be one of "little faith," and to ultimately deny his association with Jesus three times, fearing for his own safety. Yet, he was still willing to accept martyrdom in the service of the one who he had denied. Peter was crucified at Rome with his head downwards, as he had desired to suffer. This is why an upside down cross is generally accepted as a symbol of Peter, who did not consider himself worthy enough to die the same way as his Savior. Why would Peter deny his master and then end up willingly dying in His service?

Andrew was Peter's brother and a fisherman whom Christ called away from his livelihood to become a "fisher of men." He is said to have been martyred by crucifixion at the city of Patras in Achaea. Andrew was bound, rather than nailed, to a Latin cross of the kind on which Jesus is said to have been crucified; another tradition developed that Andrew had been crucified on an X-shaped cross now known as a "Saint Andrew's Cross" — supposedly at his own request, as he also deemed himself unworthy to be crucified on the same type of cross as Jesus had been.

Agrippa I had James executed by sword. He is the only apostle whose martyrdom is recorded in the New Testament and he is believed to have been the first martyred for Christ. James, one of the "Sons of Thunder" who was rebuked by Jesus for wanting to call down fire on a Samaritan town, was one of only three to bear witness to the Transfiguration.

Philip and Bartholomew were also crucified upside-down. Philip c o n t i n u e d t o p r e a c h f r o m his cross . Because of Philip's preaching, the crowd released Bartholomew from his cross, but Philip insisted that they not release him, and he was stoned while still hanging upside down on the cross.

Bartholomew is said to have been martyred in Albanopolis in Armenia. After the trial and crucifixion of Christ, Bartholomew continued to travel throughout the region and preach the gospel.   He made to modern day Armenia where he converted the king to Christianity and was killed by the king's brother.   Some histories have him as being beheaded while others contend that he was flayed while still alive and crucified with his head downward.

Matthew, the tax collector who invited Jesus to his home, much to the consternation of the Pharisees, ended up preaching the gospel as far away as Ethiopia. Little is known of Matthew's death, but most historians hold that he was martyred, but there is no adequate confirmation. What is known of Matthew's life after the crucifixion is that he remained a tireless disciple of Christ, with some reports having him as far west as Ethiopia and as far to the east as Persia.

Thomas, "the doubter," who would not believe in the risen Christ unless he saw the His pierced hands and put his finger in the wounds made by the nails and His spear-pierced side, was condemned to death in India, led out of the city to a hill, and pierced through with spears by four soldiers.

James the "Less," also James the Just, was sentenced to death for having violated the Torah by preaching that Jesus was the Messiah. He was arrested along many other Christians and was subsequently thrown from the walls of the temple in Jerusalem and then clubbed to death.

Simon the Zealot is believed to have traveled to Egypt, North Africa and perhaps even as far as Britain to preach the gospel of Christ. He is thought to have suffered crucifixion in Persia.

Jude, also known as Thaddeus, whose father was killed for his devotion to Christ, is reported to have suffered martyrdom along with Simon.

Judas, the betrayer of Christ for thirty pieces of silver, the disillusioned disciple who valued money, himself, his revolutionary desires for his country, more than he loved Christ. He became so overwrought with the guilt of having betrayed the innocent blood that he committed suicide.

Pagans dragged Mark, considered the founder of the Christian church in Egypt, behind a horse until his body was in shreds.

John, the other "Son of Thunder" and the beloved disciple, the only one who did not forsake Jesus during His trial and crucifixion, stood faithfully at the foot of the cross. From the cross, Jesus made John the protector and guardian of Mary, His mother. John was also given the Revelation of Jesus Christ on Patmos, detailing the future triumph of his Lord. John was the exception among the disciples, surviving his contemporary apostles and living well into his nineties, dying naturally at Ephesus in about AD 100

Lastly, Paul, formerly Saul of Tarsus, a Pharisee who studied Jewish law under the esteemed Gamaliel, was a persecutor of the early Christians and held the coats of the mob that killed the first martyr, Stephen.   Saul was converted after encountering the risen Christ on the road to Damascus and being stricken blind.   The same man who had mercilessly terrorized the followers of Jesus came to refer to himself as a servant, or even a slave, of the risen messiah.   Paul's many missionary journeys are epic in their scope.   He travelled the known world, preaching the message that he had once tried to stamp out and being persecuted as he had once persecuted others. Finally, after many years in prison, Paul was martyred himself.   As a Roman citizen, Paul was allowed the more merciful death of being beheaded, rather than crucifixion.

Sure, there have been countless individuals who have died for false causes, but these people generally don't intentionally die for what they KNOW to be a lie.   They believe they have the truth and that belief propels them to act.   If Christ did not rise on the third day, and make himself known to his disciples, the disciples would have certainly been a dispirited lot and likely would have scattered, probably searching for the "real" messiah.   But they didn't.   Their faithfulness to the "lie" of Jesus as the Messiah was amazing and amazingly stupid considering there was no upside to preaching to the world that a dead man was God. Unless, of course, they were witnesses to the fact that the man they called "Christ" was not dead. The only way that so many people would be willing to suffer persecution, torture, and death is if they knew that

He was who He said He was and that fact was proven by virtue of the Resurrection.

What Do You Do With This Knowledge?

In the end, how you get to your belief is less important than what you do with it? As it says in James,

> *Thou believest that there is one God; thou doest well: the devils also believe, and tremble.*

To be a Christian is not an intellectual exercise. It does no good to spend all your time studying the minutiae of doctrine and history if it is nothing more than ammunition for a debate. Such an approach is a lot like training for a marathon but never actually running the race. You may marvel at you own progress but its largely time wasted. While you are waiting to impress a skeptic with your great knowledge there may be a person right next door who just wants a kind word, who just needs to hear that someone loves them. Attend to their immediate needs. In the end, you always want to know more about someone you love and that loves you. However, always remember: your relationship with Christ should never be viewed as an "either/or" proposition. It's not a trade-off between reason and faith. A fully formed Christians needs full use of both aspects of their being.

So, where do we go from here? It's a little like the recording at the beginning of the old Mission Impossible television show, "Your mission, if you choose to accept it, is…" Accepting the mission changes everything. You are no longer on the sidelines, watching the game from the bench. You're in the game! By accepting the kingship of Jesus Christ, you have been set apart for His purpose, heart, and mind. You have a job to do.

Learn - He Wants Us to Know Him

How We Communicate

"My sheep listen to my voice; I know them and they follow me." (John 10:27)

You and I are in an amazing position. Why? Because the creator of the universe and everything in it wants so desperately to have a close relationship with us.   That should make you stop in wonder. God, who simply spoke EVERYTHING into existence, wants us to be his friends. That is what they mean by "friends in high places."

From the very beginning, God has sought a personal and intimate, relationship with every one of us. This is no laissez faire deity.   This is no hands-off deistic god who winds the clock, then sits back, and watches. God is not distant nor is He absent from our lives, quite the opposite. Everything about Him seeks closeness. As a God of love, he yearns to share Himself with anyone who will simply call out to Him.

James tells us that, if we draw close to God, He will draw close to us. What could be closer than an intimate conversation between two confidants? By communicating through scripture, God reveals His mind to us. By going to Him in prayer, we open our hearts to Him. By offering up our praise, we take the spirit and truth we find through prayer and scripture and join the angels around the throne of God. It is through these acts of communication that we learn about God and His will for us.

We need these points of contact with God because we human beings are a talkative species. We love to communicate with one another. In fact, cutting someone off from contact with fellow prisoners is considered a punishment in the penal system. Most of our days are spent communicating with other people, in person, on the phone, e-mail, text, fax, social media websites, and many other ways that I probably haven't even heard of yet. We even communicate by touch, by a look. One of the top reasons marriages fail? Lack of communication! People spend hundreds of dollars per hour to lie on a couch and talk to therapists. We talkers love a good listener.

Communication is how we share with one another, its how we relate to each other, and how we learn about each other. From the most complex life forms down to the simplest organism, the sharing of information is an integral part of life. In the scope of human relations, it is simply impossible to love another person and not want to communicate with them, to share information. It seems that is how we are hardwired. Perhaps this is our nature because it is also God's nature. He wants us to come to Him, to share, to talk. Moreover, he wants us to hear His voice, to listen attentively to His words of guidance, of solace, and of compassion. Again, you cannot love someone and not want to share with him or her. That is what is largely missing from our institutional Christianity: love, a love that is born of a complete surrender to our Savior. It is that surrender which is forgone in a relationship that is more about fulfilling an obligation and keeping up the tradition, than it is about the simple desire to know Christ. Love seeks a greater knowledge of its object. Love seeks to share itself with its object.

The Secret Power

I once was lost in sin, but Jesus took me in
Then a little light from heaven healed my soul
Well He bathed my heart with love
And He wrote my name above
Just a little talk with Jesus makes it right – Cleavant
Derricks

I won't lie to you; there have been times in my life that praying has been hard, it felt entirely one-sided. Sometimes it still does. Not to mention, there were times that I wondered why pray at all? Surely, God knows what I need without me telling Him. In addition, is it selfish to pray for things that I want? And another thing, when Jesus told his disciples, "when you pray, pray like this," does that mean I need to recite that verbatim every time I pray? Talking to God was getting very stressful for me, but I pressed onward, still do, because prayer is one of the most important things that we can do as Christians. I am still growing in my walk with Christ and I know that I can't expect to approach the throne of God with the same closeness as a believer who has a more mature faith, but that is my goal; to totally immerse my self, no, to leave my Self behind, and feel the complete, unhindered ecstasy of a life in Christ. Prayer is an integral part of reaching that goal.

As I said, we humans are natural communicators. Most of us want to talk. We need to share and enjoy it when others want to share with us. Again, I think this is because that is also God's nature. He created us in order to share Himself and He takes pleasure in us when we share with Him. When we pray, an intimacy does not exist in any other aspect of our Christian life. Even standing in a crowd of other people, we enter into God's presence alone. He hears just us. In the words of the 18th Century English cleric, William Law:

> *Prayer is the nearest approach to God, and the highest enjoyment of Him, that we are capable of in this life. It is the noblest exercise of the soul, the most exalted use of our best faculties, and the highest imitation of the blessed inhabitants of Heaven.*

> *When our hearts are full of God, sending up holy desires to the throne of grace, we are then in our highest state, we are upon the utmost heights of human greatness; we are not before kings and princes, but in the presence and audience of the Lord of all the world, and can be no higher, till death is swallowed up in glory.*

In the act of praying, we turn our hearts towards God and He turns His towards us.

Getting started with prayer, like most things, can require creating a habit of doing it until it becomes second nature. Not, however, an unthinking act in which you are merely going through the motions, but simply to make sure that you always set aside a time to pray. Corrie Ten Boom states that we shouldn't just pray when we feel like it, but to set aside a time and make sure we always keep it. It may be that the prayers we say when we aren't "in the mood" may be the most honest. I'm sure God would to prefer to hear the honest words of a grouch over the fake sincerity and well rehearsed prayers of a hypocrite.   We have to remember that God already knows what is in our hearts; we are not hiding anything from him. It is best to get the things we would hide out into the open, give them to God so that He can begin to move though us, to clean the stains that we would seek to bury within us.   Therefore, when you are angry, sad, cranky, feeling completely un-Christ-like, that may by the very best times to open up a dialogue with God, provided that you are honest with yourself and willing to admit to your shortcomings, repent and move on.

For many years, this was a sticking point in my life. At times it still is. I feel like I should not pray because I'm not worthy enough to go before God, to take my concerns to Him, to offer praise. Why would He want to hear from me, anyway? This is not humility or being humble, this is self- pity. This attitude is more of the "woe-is-me" cries of an attention-seeking hypochondriac than it is the sincere recognition of one's place in the eyes of the perfect, holy God of the Universe. If this is you, I will tell you the same thing that I have to tell myself from time to time: JUST DROP IT! This frame of mind has nothing to do with you and your position in relation to God; this is wedge being driven between you and Him. Prayer is one of the most basic and key aspects of a Christians' relationship with Christ and if Satan can prevent you in this act, he is already making headway in your life.

Ask yourself this question the next time you feel like you cannot or should not go to Him in prayer: If He was willing to send His own son to die to atone for our sins; do you think that he wants those same sins to keep us from even talking to Him? Therein lies the wonderful beauty of the Lord we serve, that none of us are worthy of approaching His throne and yet, through His grace, we are all welcomed there, we simply have to answer the knock at the door.

Christ gives us two very important lessons about the nature of prayer, first in his answer to the disciples about how to pray and then again with his own heartfelt prayer in Gethsemane.

The Lord's Prayer, as it is known, occurs in both gospels of Matthew and Luke and is not meant to be recited by us word-for-word, though there is nothing wrong with doing that. It is a pattern meant to show how we should relate to the God of the Universe. As I have said, it is the rare deity that seems to care about its creation and it is unique to Christianity that we have a God who is also our loving Father and seeks to be related to as such. Because He is a compassionate and altogether holy Father, we should pray that His will is extended, through us and our actions, to the earthly realm just as it is in the heavenly. That is our commission on earth and should be our greatest wish, for God to work through us to win over as many as we can and to bring about His kingdom, for His will to be done.

Our God is also a giving God and we are told that whatever we ask in His name will be done in accordance with His will:

> *Verily, verily, I say unto you, He that believeth on me, the works that I do shall he do also; and greater works than these shall he do; because I go unto my Father. And whatsoever ye shall ask in my name, that will I do, that the Father may be*

> *glorified in the Son. If ye shall ask any thing in my*
> *name, I will do it. - John 14:12*

However, God is not a genie given to us to grant our every wish upon simply rubbing a bottle. The ultimate goal is that every thing works towards His will, the fulfillment of His kingdom. Any request not in line with that goal is simply not a reasonable request. Our prayers, like everything in our lives, should be directed towards the glory of God. It must be remembered that even the petitions of Christ in Gethsemane were not granted in order that the will of God could be accomplished.

God also forgives those who have a heart that freely forgives others, as well. Our own sins, especially those we stubbornly hang onto, are a hindrance to God freely giving to us all that He desires to give. Resentment and anger towards others creates "white noise," a sort of spiritual static that can reduce the effectiveness of our prayers, and serves to keep us distant from God. We are told in 1 Peter that marital strife, such as a man failing to honor his wife as scripture tells us to do, can result in the hindrance of his prayers. God loves a contrite and humble heart, but a heart that is harboring ill feelings towards another prevents us from fully realizing all that God intends for us. He forgives us for so much that it is only reasonable that we should extend the same to those around us.

Lastly, prayer is a call for reinforcements. We have a direct line to God that we can use any time we need strength, courage, and deliverance from every day temptations to great evils. Even though we may walk through our own valleys of stress and turmoil, we need fear no evil, for the Lord is always there for us. Christ himself is an example of this.

In his moment of anguish, Jesus turned to prayer in Gethsemane. Telling his disciples that his soul was overwhelmed with sorrow to the point of death, he turned to the Father. No less than three times Jesus, with dread in his heart about what lay ahead of him, asked that the cup be taken from him. If it were possible, if there be any other way, he prayed, that the redemption of man could be accomplished without the cross, He asked that the burden be taken from Him. Nevertheless, in an act that should serve as an example to us all, he ultimately acquiesced to God's will. There would be no other way to further the Kingdom except by the blood of the lamb. The petitions of the only sinless man to ever walk the earth were denied because they did not fit God's perfect will. The next time we go to the Lord in prayer, we need to remember what it means to pray that His will be done and to accept that it may mean that we do not always get what we want in this world. All of the other statements and promises that are made about prayer need to be put into the context of Gethsemane. Christ's own petitions were denied and He accepted that His d e s i r e s w e r e s e c o n d a r y t o t h a t o f t h e F a t h e r ' s Kingdom. When we pray, therefore, we should always bear in mind that it is His will that should be the yardstick against which our requests are measured. Any that come up lacking should be discarded.

The Mind of God

We fail in our duty to study God's Word not so much because it is difficult to understand, not so much because it is dull and boring, but because it is work. Our problem is not a lack of intelligence or a lack of passion. Our problem is that we are lazy - **R.C. Sproul**

Here is a disclaimer that may save some of you a little bit of time. I believe that the Bible, all of the Bible, is the inerrant word of God. From Genesis 1:01 to Revelation 22:21, it was all given to us, largely in its current state and it is an accurate statement of the mind of God (excepting a few terrible translations). I also believe that all scripture is given by inspiration of God, and is profitable for doctrine, for reproof, for correction, for instruction in righteousness. And, more often than not, I adhere to a literal interpretation of the text, but I do acknowledge some poetic license by the authors, as well as some language that is a product of its time. If you differ with this approach to Biblical study, if you think it is too simplistic, too old-fashioned, you may want to skip this section. However, I wish you would not! I believe the Holy Bible to be a window into God's thought process. The Enlightenment thinker John Locke once said that a man's actions are the best interpreter of his thoughts. Through Scripture, we get to see God's actions, literally from the beginning of time, up unto the great conclusion of history. Through these actions, God shares His mind with all of us and gives us a peek into His eternal plan of salvation.

How many of us are living examples of R.C. Sproul's claim that I quoted at the beginning of this section: too lazy to seriously study the Bible? I am not talking about a cursory reading of a passage or even a whole chapter from time-to-time, but a structured study of the text. Who has the time? Besides, we are adults; we should not be expected to be doing homework at our age. Right? How many of us are just too intimidated by the text, by the archaic language of the King James or where to even start? We follow along with the preacher on Sunday mornings, is that not enough?

It's a sad fact that most Christians will spend countless hours devouring near pornographic romance novels, 500+ page mystery thrillers, or even book after book of "tween lit" series about wizards and vampires, but will rarely touch their Bibles or, at most, will only give it a half hour or so per week to meet some "required" reading assignment given to them at church. The responsibility of Biblical scholarship is placed squarely on the shoulders of our pastors while we sit idly by, waiting upon them to tell us what the Bible says and what it is supposed to mean. At one time, the Catholic Church feared the laity having access to the Bible out of the concern that they wouldn't be able to understand that which they read. In 1199, Pope Innocent III wrote this:

The mysteries of the faith are not to be explained rashly to anyone. Usually in fact, they cannot be understood by everyone but only by those who are qualified to understand them with informed intelligence. The depth of the divine Scriptures is such that not only the illiterate and uninitiated have difficulty understanding them, but also the educated and the gifted.

Nearly a thousand years later, the laity seems to be imposing the same restrictions upon themselves.

Many of us have a strange relationship with our Bibles. It is consistently the best selling book in the world, with sales estimates as high as 6 billion copies, and parts of it have been translated into over 2000 different languages. It always tops the lists of the most important books of all time and is always on our "desert island" reading lists, and yet so few of us really read it or read it thoroughly. We choose to read bits and pieces, here and there, out of context, and completely ignore anything too difficult or with which we might disagree. We make the text conform to our opinion by omission of anything contrary to what we already believe. As George Bernard Shaw said, No man ever believes that the Bible means what it says. He is always convinced that it says what he means. We are the filter through which we purify the Word, rather than the other way around.

Our approach to Scripture is a result of our increasingly postmodern view of truth, itself. In the Gospel of John, when Christ is brought before Pilate, Jesus claims that he has come to testify to the truth and everyone on the side of truth is on His side. Pilate's response is one that has been echoed throughout the ages and has become one of the defining traits of what researcher George Barna refers to as the "mosaic generation," those people born between 1984 and 2002. Pilate's response to Christ's claim is to question the very nature of truth. "What is truth?" Pilate asks.

With the Mosaic generation, more than at anytime in modernity, we see a refusal of any notion of objective truth, of universal morality. What is "true" depends upon the circumstances. What's "true" for you may not be "true" for me. What was "true" yesterday or in a different culture may not be "true" today, in our culture. If you ask someone in the late teens to the late Twenties, "What is truth?" the answer will almost invariably be, "Well, that all depends…" This is evident in their approach to the Bible.

Increasingly, many people are considering the Bible as just one of many holy books, one version of the "truth" that is no more or less relevant than the *Koran*, the *Book of Mormon*, or the *Vedas*, *the Bhagavad-Gita*, or even many secular "self help" books. The Bible may be your path to your "truth," but it is not the only path to the only "truth," seems to be the Mosaic zeitgeist. Granted, there is a common tendency for youth to rebel against the values and beliefs of their forbears and then eventually come to accept those values as their own. However, with the Mosaics we see a greater divide between them and the previous generation than ever before. Only 3% of the Mosaic generation believes that absolute moral truth exists and that this truth is encapsulated in the Bible. As this generation takes over and they become the guardians and gatekeepers of culture, their moral subjectivism will become the nation's character.

The fact is many of us approach the Bible with preconceived notions of what we think it should say rather than an openness and desire to receive what it does say. We seek to make Scripture conform to our own subjective morality and, in doing so; strip the text of its universality and, therefore, its value.

The Word of God is one of the primary ways in which He communicates about Himself and His plans for us. If you want to know God and what he desires for you, you absolutely have to study the Bible. There is simply no way around it and, the depth of your willingness to spend time in the Scriptures may very well gauge the depth of your relationship with Him. They are love letters for a smitten suitor to read over and over, ancient documents for a historian to pour through day in day out, rules for living that philosophers and ethicists can reflect upon endlessly, it is truly the greatest story ever told for all of us to turn to time and time again for hope and inspiration and, more than all of that, every single words declares the glory of our God. To read the Bible, to want to learn more and more about His love, should be a natural desire for all who call Christ their personal savior.

There is much to be gained by reading the whole text, cover to cover. Many of my own concerns and ideas about "contradictions" fell apart the first time I read the whole Bible. I know that many people suggest a yearlong approach that gives you small parts of Old Testament, New Testament, some Proverbs and some Psalms each day until you complete the Bible. That does not work for me; I simply lack the patience! I like to read it all in a 90-day program and then spend the rest of the year on studies of specific books or topics. Nevertheless, the year long plan works for many people and should not be discouraged. It breaks a seemingly daunting task up into "bite sized" pieces and gets you on your way to becoming acquainted with the Bible in its entirety, which is a huge first step towards a deeper knowledge of it. As for me, I agree with the words of Amos Wells:

> *You who like to play at Bible,*
> *Dip and dabble, here and there,*
> *Just before you kneel, aweary,*
> *And yawn thro' a hurried prayer;*
> *You who treat the Crown of Writings*
> *As you treat no other book*
> *Just a paragraph disjointed,*
> *Just a crude, impatient look*
> *Try a worthier procedure,*
> *Try a broad and steady view; You*
> *will kneel in very rapture When*
> *you read the Bible through.*

If, however, you are not quite ready to tackle the whole thing, start with a study of one of the Gospels and learn about the life of Christ. The gospels are a mixture of narrative and doctrine that is both exciting and informative. As Christians, we should all have an intimate knowledge of the life of our savior. The teachings, the love for all mankind, the hope of a life in Him, and the ultimate sacrifice that was paid for us; the Gospels give us the very heart of what it means to be a follower of Christ.

And remember, if you find yourself not understanding what you are reading, don't simply "double down" o n your lack of understanding. When reading fails, when reason fails; pray. We cannot even begin to understand the Word of God without His assistance in the first place. Therefore, God, as the measure of all things, must be involved when we read His word. As such, the Holy Spirit is our helper, our Virgil through the Scriptures. Lacking that animating power, we are lost and the text appears meaningless, our efforts, fruitless.

Put On the Amour

"For the time will come when they will not endure sound doctrine-2 Timothy 4:3-4

Wherever you choose to start, the important thing is that you start. We are responsible to know what is in the Scriptures ourselves and not to rely on others for our information. When God lamented in Hosea that his people were destroyed for a lack of knowledge, it wasn't that they did not know how to change a flat or bake a soufflé, it was their lack of knowledge of Him. We study scripture in order to understand, if only a small part, the unchanging mind of God. It is this knowledge, backed with faith, which forms a bulwark against our own destruction. Without it, we are defenseless. It is this knowledge that is given up when we deny objective truth and universal morality. The subjectivism of the postmodern world is tailor-made to lead us away from Christ and towards our own destruction.

We are warned many times in the Bible to beware of false teachers, those who spread false doctrine, and destructive heresies. Second Timothy warns of a coming time "when they will not endure sound doctrine...and they will turn their ears away from the truth, and be turned aside to fables." However, how will we recognize false teaching if we don't know the correct teaching? When that day comes, all will be lost if you fail to arm yourself with the "the belt of truth buckled around your waist, with the breastplate of righteousness in place, and with your feet fitted with the readiness that comes from the gospel of peace. In addition to all this, take up the shield of faith, with which you can extinguish all the flaming arrows of the evil one. Take the helmet of salvation and the sword of the Spirit, which is the word of God."

The church has fractured repeatedly and many different schism and heresies have sprung out of a poor understanding of the Bible. Throughout the ages, mankind has committed all manners of atrocities and innumerable numbers of men and women have died due to our unwillingness to consistently approach the Scriptures with a humble heart and an inquisitive mind. One false teacher can lead many who do not know any better to ruin.

You are Worthy of My Praise

Praising God may be the most natural of things in the whole universe. To give the Creator of all things an acknowledgment of His glory seems self-evident. If the stones were apt to cry out in praise as Jesus entered Jerusalem, how much more should we, His children, raise our voices to Him? How much more should we sing of His eternal glory? When Adam fell, we were torn from our original state, and our sin nature stands as a gulf separating us from the closeness that God had intended. Our inclination to praise is a testament to our soul's longing to ascend towards Him in whose image it was made. We offer up our praise because He deserves it, because that is why we were created, because there should be no other desire when faced with the glory of God.

Of course, when I speak of praise I am not referring to the songs we sing together on Sunday mornings. Those are merely vehicles, a medium. Praise is our grateful and humble recognition of God for who He is; an acknowledgement of the glory of Jesus Christ and the eternal debt we owe to Him. It is less of an act than it is an attitude.

The 18th Psalm tells us that God is "worthy to be praised." Why? First and foremost, He is worthy to be praised for the gift of life through Jesus Christ. If we had no other knowledge of God except that of the cross, He would still merit more praise than we could ever give Him. He loved the infinitely unlovable, took all of our worst upon Himself so that we might enjoy a life in Him. We are the recipients of a gift, freely given, and completely undeserved. For this, we praise Him.

We praise Him in recognition of His holiness. In 1 John, we are told that God is light; in Him there is no darkness at all. He is the source of all holiness and through Him we are sanctified, set aside for His holy purposes. We give Him praise for providing a way out of the darkness of this world into the light of eternal joy with Him. Because He is holy, we also may be holy. For this, we praise Him.

We praise Him because He is sovereign. All things are in His control, either directed by Him or allowed by Him. In Him, we can have complete trust for we know that His plans are to prosper us, to provide us with the ultimate gift of life everlasting. In Proverbs we are told, "Many are the plans in man's heart but it is the Lord's purpose that prevails" and His purpose is to cover our sins with His perfect love. For this, we praise Him.

We praise Him because of His unfailing love, a love that reaches to the heavens. Through His love, our sin is atoned for and we are saved. His love is the ultimate source of all love. By Him, we are able to love each other as we share in this divine attribute by being made in His image. Through Him, all love is possible. For this, we praise Him.

We praise God because of His perfect righteousness. Scripture tells us that He loves justice and His awesome deeds of righteousness are the hope of all the earth. Our Lord will be exalted by His justice, and God will show Himself holy by His righteousness. In Him alone are righteousness and strength. All who have raged against Him will be put to shame. For this, we praise Him.

We praise Him because of His faithfulness. The Psalmist tells us that, even if we are faithless, God remains faithful. It is His nature. Those who wait on the Lord shall inherit the earth and shall delight in an abundance of peace that flows from His divine goodness. He is the faithful God who keeps His covenant for a thousand generations with those who love Him and keep His commandments. In Deuteronomy, it is written that the eyes of the Lord run to and fro throughout the whole earth, to show Himself strong on behalf of those whose heart is loyal to Him. The Lord keeps His promises. For this, we praise Him.

Moreover, we praise Him for the countless things that He has done in our own lives. I praise Him for His patience, that no matter how often I fail, He is always ready to forgive. I praise Him for the hope that He gives me, for the strength that I find in Him. I praise Him for the wonderful gift of my wife and the children that He has entrusted to me. I praise Him that I was born in a country where I am free to praise Him! For the fellowship of believers who have been my support in bad times and with whom I have shared the joy of the Lord at all times. For the material blessings that have been provided. And, again, if for no other reason than that of gift of salvation through Jesus Christ, for these things, I praise Him.

In good times and in bad, we should praise Him for all this and so much more.

Too often we delay our praise, holding out for more, wanting more, thinking we deserve more and then, only then, do we think that we should offer up praise. Rather than acknowledging the many gifts we have already received, we hoard our praise like misers only to lose it. Our ability to praise, like an unused limb, begins to atrophy, to become shriveled with selfishness and greed. Our spirit becomes stultified as we drag ourselves further and further away from God. Our soul is made to praise, to ascend on wings of thanksgiving to the Throne of the Savior, but our mind, our ego, keeps chaining it down with the desires of the world. The longer it remains earthbound the less likely it will be able to take flight again.

He is worthy of my praise even when I don't feel like giving it, those times when I let my own selfish concerns and the cares of this world get in between me and Him. It is in those moments that I sometimes feel furthest from him; when I'm tired, stressed about work, when my wife and I have had a fight, when I'm withdrawn and concerned only about myself. It is in those times that I like to think of God as the loving Father, who is standing close to me and saying, "Yeah, I get it. I know what you're feeling and its okay. This world is not the world that I had intended for you. But, if you just turn your focus to me, I'll get you through it." I must remember to praise Him through the dark nights of the soul and to let Him do the rest. By praising Him, even in my dark, solitary moods, I move closer to Him and He changes me. As C.S. Lewis put it: "It is in the process of being worshipped that God communicates His presence to men." In feeling that presence, one need never feel alone.

Live - He Expects Us to Live by His Example

From the Heart

Do nothing out of selfish ambition or vain conceit, but in humility consider others better than yourselves. 4 Each of you should look not only to your own interests, but also to the interests of others. 5 Your attitude should be the same as that of Christ Jesus. - Philippians 2:3-5 - 3

Too many people are being turned off by the church, not because of doctrine or lack of a willingness to believe, but by Christians themselves. As the saying goes, "I like Jesus; it's his followers that I can't stand." Many of us in the church appear as either holier-than-thou prudes who look down on everyone as "Sinners." Alternatively, we are WINO's, Witnesses in Name Only, Christians who put a fresh coat of paint on every Sunday morning but are indistinguishable from the world the other six days of the week. Rather than being set aside for God's purpose, we do our best to fit in, to conform to the world around us. The result being that our personal hypocrisy taints many people's opinion of the entire body of Christ.

Such is the state of the institutional Christian, the DMV Christian. To those who have a genuine relationship with Christ, to conform to the world is to break a covenant, to be an unfaithful bride. To the WINO's, all obligations are fulfilled by the simple act of weekly church attendance. God has no claim on our actions for the other 6 days of the week. We have given God His time; the rest of the week is ours.

Much like a wedding ring is a statement to the world that we are "off the market," our actions should be a similar pronouncement to the world; that we are His and therefore not wedded to the things of this world. Once you acknowledge the kingship of Christ, you are a representative of Him. And as a representative, He expects us to appropriately represent Him to the world, to be the living embodiment of the one who has saved us so that others will want to know the source of our happiness. To do any less is to defame God. In the words of theologian J.I. Packer:

> *"God's call to be holy, as he is holy, is a general summons to live by his revealed precepts and prohibitions, as embodying the loves and hates which make up his character and which his ways*

> *with us will always express; Christ's call to follow his example is a specific summons to unlimited self-humbling, and giving of ourselves without restraint, in order to relieve others' needs and make them great, which is what true love is all about."*

The image of God that the world knows is largely that which is provided by His followers. What sort of image are we creating in their eyes by our actions? Is it one of love and hope, of forgiveness and a humble heart? On the other hand, is it condemnation, of being judgmental? Is it one of hypocrisy and double standards, where we say one thing on Sunday mornings and do something entirely different the rest of the week? I know that I have too often failed to practice what it is that I preach, that I talk of the Kingdom but live as the world. The process of sanctification, of becoming more Christ-like in our character, is a lifelong process, but we must accept that we play a role in that process. We are not lifeless clay in God's hands. We make daily choices that either aid or hinder the process and those around us are witness to our triumphs and our failures.

Freed from the Law…

Jesus answered them, "Truly, truly, I say to you, everyone who commits sin is the slave of sin. "The slave does not remain in the house forever; the son does remain forever. "So if the Son makes you free, you will be free indeed. – Matthew 8:34-36

One of the main themes of the New Testament is freedom. We have been loosed from the bonds of the flesh, of sin, and of the Law. By the time of Jesus, the Jewish people were under enough rules and regulations to make a modern day bureaucrat wince. The Ten Commandments handed to Moses on Mount Sinai had grown into a web of regulations that covered everything from how to properly observe holy days to the treatment of animals and what you can and cannot wear. It also established the requirements of caring for the poor, proper social interactions and the need for atonement for sins by a blood sacrifice. It is generally accepted that there are 613 commandments established in the Torah, which is significant because 613 is the numerical value of the word "Torah" plus two added for the two commandments that existed prior ("I am the Lord your God" and "You shall have no other God before me"). There were also "Rabbinic Laws," commandments not established in the Torah but enacted by rabbis under the authority to make judgments about the Law as expressed in Deuteronomy. On top of these were various customs that, due largely to their longevity, were eventually accepted as law, as well.

One wonders how the average Jew in the time of Christ could even know all of the laws, let alone observe them all. Here is just a small sample of the laws related to the proper treatment of animals:

> *Because our domesticated animals depend upon us for sustenance, they should be fed before us.*

You may feed animals non-kosher food unless the food consists of a mixture of meat and milk cooked together. This is not allowed.

It is forbidden to feed your animals food containing leaven on the Passover.

On the Sabbath and holidays it is forbidden to feed stray animals, except for dogs.

It is forbidden to feed animals food that is fit for human consumption because that is disrespectful to the bounty that G-d has given us. However, if the food is leftover a n d will o t h e r w i s e b e discarded, it may be fed to animals.

And here is a little of the Law of the Morning Routine:

To express gratitude, before getting out of bed, you should say the following prayer: "I thank Thee, O living and eternal King, because Thou hast graciously restored my soul to me; great is Thy faithfulness." It is okay to say this prayer prior to the washing of the hands because the name of G-d isn't mentioned in it.

As soon as you awaken you should get out of bed so that evil inclinations do not sway you from serving your Creator.

Upon rising, you must purify yourself and wash your hands from a vessel. When a man is asleep, unclean spirits descend upon him and the spirit does not depart from him unless he spills water on his hands three times alternately.

One is not permitted to walk four cubits before washing his hands.

The growth of the Law and the impossibility of adhering to it, rather than bringing the people closer to God, had become a weight upon them. It is no wonder that Christ promised them that His yoke was easy; the Jewish people would have been a receptive audience to the message of such a spiritual liberation.

The fact is that the Law was never meant to be the final word between God and man. The Law was a spotlight on our nature as humans, on the sin imbedded in every one of us. Moreover, it was meant to show the hopelessness of any effort on our own to achieve righteousness. The ever expanding number of rules and requirements that covered every aspect of their daily lives was simply too much to bear. The law was hopelessness and despair, but it allowed them to see that there could be no hope of salvation through their own actions. As Paul says in his epistle to the Romans, the law is the knowledge of sin and death, from which the law of the spirit of life in Jesus has released us.

In the end, the law simply controlled people's actions but had no effect on their hearts. The law had become a dry, lifeless thing that offered little hope. This is why Christ showed so much anger towards the Pharisees, the religious leaders of the day who called upon the people to follow the laws strictly. Repeatedly, Jesus calls the Pharisees out for appearing outwardly righteous but being full of hypocrisy and iniquity, for pursuing the practice of the law but ignoring the "weightier matters of the law, judgment, mercy, and faith." How it must have stung the Pharisees to hear Christ tell the people that unless their righteousness EXCEEDS that of the Pharisees that they shall not enter into the Kingdom of Heaven. These men, the arbiters of what was good and holy, were being held up as examples of how NOT to live. The Pharisees had evolved into their own brand of DMV faith, their own birthright religion simply because they were descendants of Abraham. Jesus dashed this ancestral claim to righteousness:

> And think not to say within yourselves, we have Abraham to our father; for I say unto you, that God is able of these stones to raise up children to Abraham.

In response, these men, these religious leaders of the day, sought the death of Jesus Christ. Often our own ideas of God are dearer to us than He is Himself. We become our own law; we become Pharisees in our hearts and are more concerned about outward appearances than we are about our inner voice that simply cries out for the person of Jesus. Or, relying upon an "ancestral" claim to righteousness (an institutional Christianity), we exhibit a faith that fails to measure up to stones. Perhaps our faith is even less than that of simple rocks. We are told that these rocks would have been unable to contain themselves and would have cried out to praise Jesus had the people not done so, as he made His triumphal entry into Jerusalem. Sometimes my own weak faith makes me embarrassed when I consider those rocks.

The Kingdom and the Ultimate Sacrifice

The teachings of Christ were revolutionary in that he moved beyond salvation through deeds and ritual observances as prescribed by the law and established that salvation depended upon accepting the gift of grace that he freely gave to all, a grace made possible by his atonement as a sacrifice for all. This is what he meant when he said that he came not to overturn the law, but to fulfill it. He did not end the law; he brought it to its intended, ultimate culmination. It always pointed towards him. It is not that He came after the law, but that the law was a shadowy precursor of what was to come; the foundation for the Kingdom of God was being built at the foot of the cross. It says in Hebrews:

> For the law, having a shadow of the good things to come, and not the very image of the things, can never with these same sacrifices, which they offer continually year by year, make those who approach perfect. For then would they not have ceased to be offered? For the worshipers, once purified, would have had no more consciousness of sins. But in those sacrifices there is a reminder of sins every year. For it is not possible that the blood of bulls and goats could take away sins.

103

Every year, atonement was made for the transgressions of the Jewish people. This day, still the holiest day of the year for the Jews, is known as The Day of Atonement or Yom Kippur. Yom meaning "day" and Kippur translates as either "to cover" or "to expiate." On this day, their collective sins were placed upon one "sinless animal" that was sacrificed in the temple, its blood collected and then taken by the high priest through the veil which only he could go, and placed upon an altar in the Holy of Holies, where the Ark of the Covenant had once set and where the very presence of God was said to come down.. According to the law, this was an acceptable offering for the sins of the people of the Jewish nation. However, after the destruction of the Second Temple by the Romans in 70AD, the sacrifices were no longer possible. It is said that Rabbi Yochanan ben Zakkai, one of the primary contributors to the Mishnah, was walking near the ruins of the Temple with one of his students when the student cried out, "Alas for us! The place that atoned for the sins of the people Israel lies in ruins!" With no temple, no Holy of Holies, there could be no sacrifice, no atonement. Based upon the teachings of Zakkai and other religious leaders, scripture was interpreted that the Jewish people could seek atonement in acts of charity and kindness in the absence of the temple sacrifices. They based this on passages such as:

> *"Doing charity and justice is more desirable to the Lord than sacrifice" (Proverbs 21:3).*

Atonement is also possible by studying the High Priest's ritual and adhering to rules of conduct (fasting, not eating, driving, observing a strict day of rest, etc...). Many synagogues still act out the sacrifice of the animal and the sprinkling of blood on the altar.

However, what they fail to recognize is that Christ was that atonement, the expiation of all our sins, once and for all. It was not possible that the blood of bulls and goats could take away our sins but it is possible that the blood of Christ could, for all sins ever committed or yet to be committed. The law, the requirements and restrictions, the acts of atonement were fulfilled by the life, death, and resurrection of Jesus Christ. As Paul writes in Romans, one man (Adam) brought sin into the world and one man (Jesus) provided us a way out of that sin. One need only to accept his holy sacrifice, his gift of grace and no further acts of sacrifice are needed. The price was paid for all, forevermore. Therein lay the significance of the tearing of the veil that separated the Holy of Holies. No longer was God's presence limited to just the High Priest.

When Jesus died on the cross, many amazing events occurred. There was an earthquake, darkness in the middle of the day, tombs were thrown open, and the bodies of the saints that "slept," arose. But, the most significant event was that the mighty curtain through which only the High Priest could access the Holy of Holies was torn down the middle, from top to bottom. It is impossible to imagine what the temple priests must have felt upon seeing this happen. No one was allowed through that veil except for the High Priest and he was only able to go through it on one day of the year, the Day of Atonement, the day that sins were washed away by the blood of sacrifice. Anyone else who went through the curtain, or if the High Priest went through on the wrong day or if he failed to properly perform the rituals that accompanied going into the Holy of Holies, they were struck dead. Access was limited to one man, on one day, under very limited circumstances. But no more! Christ became our sacrifice and our High Priest. Through Him, we were allowed access to God anytime. The rending of the veil released us from the law, from death, and from any earthly mediators between God and man. As Paul writes in Romans, sin was no longer our master, for we no longer lived under the law. Instead, we lived under the freedom of God's grace. Jesus was now our only mediator. His blood was our only atonement. Nothing more was needed.

...But Not Lawless

So, if our actions are no longer guided by the prohibitions and requirements of the law, what defines Christian character? Russian writer Fyodor Dostoevsky is attributed with saying that without God, everything is permissible. In reality, Dostoevsky did not make that statement. However, one of his characters, Ivan Karamazov, d i d s a y the following: "If there is n o immortality, there is no virtue." This passage *from The Brothers Karamazov was* restated by Existentialist philosopher, Jean Paul Sartre in his essay, "Existentialism is Humanism":

> *Dostoevsky once wrote, "If God did not exist, everything would be permitted"; and that, for existentialism, is the starting point. Everything is indeed permitted if God does not exist, and man is in consequence forlorn, for he cannot find anything to depend upon either within or outside himself.*

Are all things also permissible without the guiding hand of the law, as long as it is done with love? On the other hand, can we try so hard to avoid being judgmental that we end up being tolerant of sin? This is the path we have to walk as Christians: to avoid the legalism of the law and the judgmental attitude that so often accompanies it, but not to veer off into an "anything goes" liberalism that replaces God with a love that is more about societal acceptance than it is about the character of Christ.

Often we elevate social mores or personal preferences to the level of the law and hold to these things simply because we have a personal distaste or favor for certain behaviors. Rather than loving the sinner and hating the sin, we sometimes dismiss the sin or compartmentalize it in order to stay on friendly terms with the sinner. Loving the sinner has been replaced with being the sinner's buddy and, in order to stay friends, we rationalize their sins away. In the end, rather than trying to gently lead a friend to repentance and to Christ, we make their sin disappear in a puff of relativism. It is an easy step to do

107

this for our friends when we are so well practiced in doing it for ourselves. I had several friends in college who were homosexuals; it was hard to consider the immorality of their lifestyle when I was sexually promiscuous myself. Acknowledging the sins of others would only serve to shine the light on my own sins, so between a choice of being an inconsistent hypocrite or accepting that I was no better than the people I was pointing my finger at, it was best to simply disregard it all. You turn a blind eye to me and I will do the same for you. Rather than being honest and repentant and possibly alienating friends, we choose to hang onto our sins at the expense of our relationship to Christ.

Nonbelievers and liberal or "progressive" Christians tend to have a similar approach in this regard. They base their belief system around an issue, or a feeling, about something that they actually value more than they value the existence of God and/or His nature. Often these two types of people and their attitude towards God overlap with some variant of the following declaration: I cannot believe in a God who will not let me (or someone I know) do X! With "X", being a preconceived judgment of right and wrong based on beliefs that the individual brings to the table before they even take up the issue of God.

So, if a person has a heartfelt conviction that , for example, homosexuality is okay, then the statement becomes something like: I can't believe in a God who won't let me express my love how I want and with whom I want! Similarly, a liberal Christian with liberal views of homosexuality will either simply disregard the scriptural condemnation or will beat and strangle the text until it says whatever they want it to say.

The fallacy with the atheist's position is something of a straw man. True enough, God is a god of love, but real love, not the man-made, pseudo-love that they have created in order to justify any human behavior that they may decide its okay to indulge in. Essentially, the atheist's position is to say, "I want what I want and if God says otherwise, I will usurp his throne and exile Him".

The liberal Christian accepts God in a piecemeal fashion and takes it upon himself to improve upon God's work as he sees fit. He tells God that he will accept Him in areas of agreement and disregard Him in any areas of conflict. God must change, not the believer. As such, the liberal Christian deems himself worthy to co- manage the universe with God.

Ultimately, these two groups have one thing in common; they start with themselves and create the universe from their own ideas of right and wrong. Then, and only then, do they squeeze God into whatever room is left.

On the other extreme, we can become so tied up in regulating behavior, our own and that of others, that the freedom that Christ died for was in vain. We have set up our own law and established ourselves as Pharisees: overseers of the institutional Christianity, often holding others to a higher standard than we hold ourselves, concerning ourselves with the speck in our brother's eye, oblivious to plank in our own.

Case in point: one would think, from most Christians, that all alcohol consumption is prohibited, which its not. What is condemned is over use, gluttony. However, you rarely hear about the gluttons in the pews who consume 10,000 calories per meal and have never even seen the inside of a gym. Which is a sin: moderate, responsible use of alcohol or gluttony of anything? Odds are you are much more likely to hear a sermon about the dangers of alcohol use, ANY use, than you are about people who spend too much money shopping, eat to much, work too much, etc... Because we all like to eat, we all like to acquire new stuff, we all have to put in more and more hours, even if it is at the expense of our family, but only THEY drink. Rather than offending the corpulent deacon who eats more in one meal than many under-privileged children eat in a week, let's jump on the teetotaler bandwagon. Granted, Paul does condemn drunkenness (1Timothy 3:8, Ephesians 5:18). In addition, Titus 1:7 states that a minister of God should not be given to wine or be an alcoholic. However, Paul also tells Timothy to add wine to his diet for his health (1Timothy 5:23). But, again, so many in the church today are more concerned about mores and appearances than they are with the actual text. So, they point the finger of blanket condemnation at all drinkers, no matter how responsible and moderate, and ignore the more socially acceptable forms of gluttony. It is easy to point the finger at the obvious "them" rather than the more delicate "us" when it comes to crossing perceived Biblical boundaries.

Ultimately, it becomes less about what the Word of God says and more about what we want it to say, what we think is right or wrong. We throw the sort of stumbling blocks in front of other believers that Paul refers to in Romans 14 that do nothing but complicate their and our own walk with Christ unnecessarily. One person may choose to abstain while another chooses not to abstain. Paul uses the example of choosing to follow a strict vegetarian diet, but it should be noticed that he points to the believer who chooses to abstain as being the one "whose faith is weak," not the one who doesn't abstain. Is this a coincidence or is it that the freedom of Christ relegates such matters to that of a purely personal choice based on one's own faith? We are also told that, while one person may consider a day holy, it is not a sin for another to not hold that same day as sacred. The important thing is that, whatever you choose to do in these matters, you do so for the Lord and it is an act of conscience, for you alone, guided by the Holy Spirit. It is not, however, our role to police the walk of others according to the pace and direction of our own. The key is to be aware of the weakness of your brothers and sisters and to neither cajole them into becoming a clone of ourselves nor to let our freedom be their hindrance. As C.S., Lewis writes:

> Of course, it may be the duty of a particular Christian, or of any Christian, at a particular time, to abstain from strong drink, either because he is

111

the sort of man who cannot drink at all without drinking too much, or because he wants to give the money to the poor, or because he is with people who are inclined to drunkenness and must not encourage them by drinking himself. But the whole point is that he is abstaining, for a good reason, from something which he does not condemn and which he likes to see other people enjoying. One of the marks of a certain type of bad man is that he cannot give up a thing himself without wanting every one else to give it up. That is not the Christian way.

Nevertheless, in the end, we have to remember that our own freedom can be a stumbling block to ourselves if we do not act responsibly and with concern and compassion to those around us.   Just because we have the freedom to do something, that does not mean that we should. As Paul says in 1 Corinthians, all things may be allowed, but not all things are helpful to us.   The ultimate goal of our lives is to be Christ-like and to lead others to the Him, so all our actions should be weighed with that in mind: does it advance His kingdom?   Does it edify or does it denigrate? In the end, we should always remember that our goal is to be an example of His image to the world, not to try to reshape those around us into our image.

How are we to Act?

So, what are the scriptural parameters of Christian conduct? If I may borrow and re-engineer a phrase from Paul, work out your own sanctification with love and thanksgiving for it is the Lord that works in and through you. Right conduct is possible through our own conscious effort, directed and empowered by the Holy Spirit. This aspect of sanctification, that is the practical separation unto God, is a moment-by-moment willful act wherein we allow the volitional force of the Holy Spirit to set our will into accordance with that of God and, in doing so, to put on the character of Christ, to be, in Peter's words, "partakers of the divine nature."

The 115th Psalm tells us of those who build idols in their own image, those who build dead, lifeless things, only to end up like the thing they worship: ears that cannot hear eyes that cannot see, mouths that cannot speak. But, as we saw in the previous section on praise, Christians worship the attributes of God, attributes that we can hope to share since we are made in His image. Things like forgiveness, love, holiness, etc... by worshipping Him we take on the character of the Living God, not those of a lifeless thing onto which we project our sinful selves.

A simple encapsulation of the idea of Christian character is in 2 Peter. Knowledge of God grants to us "everything pertaining to life and godliness" and it is our proper response to the "precious and magnificent promises" of Christ that we diligently:

> *...add to your faith virtue, to virtue knowledge, to knowledge self-control, to self-control perseverance, to perseverance godliness, to godliness brotherly kindness, and to brotherly kindness love. For if these things are yours and abound, you will be neither barren nor unfruitful in the knowledge of our Lord Jesus Christ.*

Our diligence is simply rising to the call, answering the knock at the door to allow Christ into our hearts. This is not the one-time acceptance of salvation, but the daily willingness to continually strive to act as an earthly representative of the Heavenly Father. To erect the character that is built, brick by brick, by every choice we make. The initial resolution to acknowledge Christ as our savior establishes the foundation of our Christian character, but our every act, every decision from that point on erects the rest of the structure before the eyes of our fellow man. It creates either a house of refuge or a house of horrors in their eyes. It may still stand upon the solid foundation of the saving grace of Jesus Christ, but it is our diligence that helps to determine if it is a shining house upon a hill or a shack only suitable for demolition.

Appropriately, Peter begins his list of virtues with faith. All of the other attributes that we should aspire to are impossible without faith. Paul tells us in Romans that whatever does not originate through faith is a sin. Also, notice that we do not add or supply faith; God gives it to us. Faith comes by hearing the word of God; again, we are taken back to the simple act of communicating with God and the fruits of a deep knowledge of Christ through studying the Scripture and going to Him in prayer and with praise.

Then, through this given faith, we are to supply moral excellence. To understand what is meant by this, we can look to Philippians where Paul tells us to let our minds dwell on only the things that are true, honorable, right and pure, lovely, of good repute, things that are worthy of praise. One cannot expect to be spiritually healthy with a diet of unhealthy habits, any more than you can hope to be physically healthy when you only eat junk food. Christ tells us that it is not what goes in a man's mouth that makes him unclean, but what comes out.   Our words, the expression of our thoughts and our heart, are the product of who we are as a person, which is greatly influenced by what we allow in; what we see, what we hear. Our food may not make us unclean but the television shows, the movies, the music, and books that we spend our time and money on, will begin to shape our mind and, through our mind, our actions. We are what we consume and, if our diet consists of garbage, we will become creatures of filth.

In Romans, we see what can become of such people, those who give themselves over to uncleanness and the things of the world, rather than those of God:

God gave them up to vile passions. For even

their women exchanged the natural use for what is against nature. Likewise also, the men, leaving the natural use of the woman, burned in their lust for one another, men with men committing what is shameful, and receiving in themselves the penalty of their error which was due. And even as they did not like to retain God in their knowledge, God gave them over to a debased mind, to do those things which are not fitting; being filled with all unrighteousness, sexual immorality, wickedness, covetousness, maliciousness; full of envy, murder, strife, deceit, evil-mindedness; they are whisperers, backbiters, haters of God, violent, proud, boasters, inventors of evil things, disobedient to parents undiscerning, untrustworthy, unloving, unforgiving, unmerciful; who, knowing the righteous judgment of God, that those who practice such things are deserving of death, not only do the same but also approve of those who practice them.

Consider Paul's final statement in that passage: not only those who do the same, but also approve of those who practice them. To condone, to tolerate the sin of others, to justify it is just as sinful as actually doing it. Loving the sinner and hating the sin is not the same as loving the sinner and turning a blind eye to sin. Tacit complicity in iniquity is n o less damnable that being an a c t i v e participant.

This practice of moral excellence will then lead to knowledge. This knowledge is a twofold pursuit. First, the knowledge that comes from the study of the Bible, the "practical" knowledge that comes from a daily immersion into the Word, a sort of exegetical baptism.   Without a dedication to reading the Bible, it is nearly impossible to know God; His characters, attributes, plans, are all laid out in those 66 books. As well, we find our responsibilities, our hope, the source of our wisdom, of our faith, and our strength.

The second type of knowledge that comes from moral excellence is the experiential knowledge of God.   The pursuit of moral excellence separates us more and more from the world and allows us to draw nearer to God.   In Colossians, Paul tells us that, by walking in the manner worthy of the Lord, we gain greater knowledge of God and that then strengthens us according to His glorious might. This strength gives the next of Peter's virtues, self-control.

Self control is a weapon in the battle of our spirit against our flesh, our earthly will and its desire to cage our soul behind bars of lust.   Christ has freed us from death, from the flesh, but our sinful nature still draws us towards it. Even when we are well aware that what we are doing is wrong, we often find ourselves in the same position as Paul, "for what I would, that do I not; but what I hate, that do I." Peter compares those without self-control to "unreasoning animals, born as creatures of instinct to be captured and killed." Without self-control, we are barely above the animals, driven by base desires to satisfy our fleshly wants, with little regard to the consequences. And we are all subject to this, we all have our vices that we are at war with almost daily, be it sex, food, drugs, gambling, spending money we don't have, our temper, laziness, our tendency to gossip, any number of things that feed the monster of the Self, of our ego, of our drive to satiate our physical cravings at the expense of our spiritual needs. Only by leaning on the self-control that comes from the knowledge of God can we hope to make our body a slave to grace.

Out of this knowledge of God and the constant battle to control he s e l f , c o m e s p e r s e r v e r a n c e , t h e ability to continue to fight the good fight, even in the face of a world that mocks us, belittles us, and would assist in our destruction. No where does Christ tell us that a life lived for him will be an easy one, but we are to forge on, knowing that, as Paul writes in Romans, the God of patience and consolation will grant us to be likeminded one toward another according to Christ Jesus. We are told that many run the race but only those who persevere to the end will win the prize. Moreover, by persevering, we can achieve godliness: character marked by a constancy of reverence that seeks to please God in all things. The newness of our life in Christ is manifested in our deeds as well as our words. We no longer simply talk the talk; we walk in His footsteps.

As this godliness grows in us, it seeks out the same in others. The body of Christ, the church, should be made up of many, acting as one, working together with a shared purpose and a God-inspired sense of fellowship. God intended for us to care for each other, to help each when in need, to strengthen and support each other. We are all equal in His eyes so we should look upon one another as an extension of ourselves, and as fellow children of God. As this brotherly kindness takes root, the love of God begins to extend to all. His love should be evident in us so that the world sees it.

God is love and he makes all love possible. Through this, we are able to see more of God's character and more of the character traits that we should emulate. In 1 Corinthians, Paul writes:

> *"Love is patient, love is kind. It does not envy, it does not boast, it is not proud. It is not rude, it is not self-seeking, it is not easily angered, it keeps no record of wrongs. Love does not delight in evil but rejoices with the truth. It always protects, always trusts, always hopes, always perseveres. Love never fails"*

These are the aspects of love because they are the character of God. Moreover, since they are the character of God, they are what we should aspire to: a life in which our relationships with others are shaped by the example of the love of God. If anyone's knowledge of God fails to progress to the ultimate goal of love, they are, in the words of Peter:

> *...shortsighted, even to blindness, and has forgotten that he was cleansed from his old sins*

.Therefore, brethren, be even more diligent to make your call and election sure, for if you do these things you will never stumble; for so an entrance will be supplied to you abundantly into the everlasting kingdom of our Lord and Savior Jesus Christ.

Simply put, to know God is to love; to love God is to present yourself as a living sacrifice to Him.

The Martyrdom of the Self

History is replete with men and women who have lain down their lives in the name of Jesus Christ. Many went as peaceful martyrs in the image of Christ himself, the Lamb of God. Others went out in a blaze of "glory," often more concerned with their own image to world than with presenting a n accurate image of God to mankind. However, God does not call us all to be literal martyrs. Sure, it has happened and will continue to happen that speaking the Word of God will result in the deaths of many of His children, especially as the world becomes increasingly more violent and filled with the spirit of the anti-Christ. However, we are not asked to seek out our own demise. It's quite the opposite, actually.

Jesus Christ stands as the ultimate martyr, the one who sacrificed everything and gave all for the express goal that all be saved. He willingly chose the earthly torments of the cross and the spiritual agony of separation from the Father so that we do not have to. In return, we are to offer ourselves as "living sacrifices" in His name. In Romans 12, Paul says this:

> ...beseech you therefore, brethren, by the mercies of God, that ye present your bodies a living sacrifice, holy, acceptable unto God, which is your reasonable service.
>
> And be not conformed to this world: but be ye transformed by the renewing of your mind, that ye may prove what is the good, and acceptable, and perfect, will of God.

As a living sacrifice, we place ourselves upon the altar daily, moment by moment as we serve God. In Exodus, we are told of what happens when the sacrificial offering is laid upon the altar:

> Seven days thou shalt make atonement for the altar, and sanctify it; and it shall be an altar most holy: whatsoever toucheth the altar shall be holy.

To sacrifice oneself or, more accurately, one's Self, by denying your sinful nature which manifests itself in your desire to pursue your own selfish interests, and to present your bodies (mind, spirit and physical) in service to God, is to die and be regenerated daily, moment by moment, which is what Paul refers to as our "reasonable service" as Christians: the constant process of sanctification. In this way, every act places our self upon the altar to be made holy.

This act of sacrifice, this service that is our reasonable

response to that of Christ himself, is the practical aspect of the process of sanctification. We are already set apart, designated as His, when we accept Him into our lives as out Lord and Savior, but our daily response to this gift continues this as we remove ourselves from this world, as we strive not to be conformed to the fallen, but rather to conform to His will so that the fallen may see Him through us. As we read in the Gospel of John, our sacrifice of ourselves is part of our purpose for the Kingdom as was Christ's own sacrifice:

> *As Thou didst send Me into the world, even so send I them into the world. And for their sakes I sanctify Myself, that they themselves also may be sanctified in truth.*

Our martyrdom is that of the Self. Whereas we were once separated from God and dying in the world, we are now separated from the world and alive in God.

Love - He Wants Us to Take His Message to the World

Therefore go and make disciples of all nations, baptizing them in the name of the Father and of the Son and of the Holy Spirit, and teaching them to obey everything I have commanded you.—Mathew 19:20

Why Are We Here?

The temple of Delphi in Greece was home to one of the most revered oracles of the ancient world. She would go into a trance and her spirit would become possessed by the god Apollo who would make pronouncements through her. The temple was a major site for the worship of Apollo, the god of, among other things, knowledge. So important was Delphi that it was considered the "omphalos," the "bellybutton of the world," the center of existence.

123

Inscribed in the marble of the temple at Delphi was the maxim, "know thyself." This call to self-awareness was attributed to everyone from Socrates to Pythagoras and Heraclites. To begin the journey of enlightenment, one must engage in a fair amount of navel-gazing. Know thyself, the Greeks said, and your purpose would follow after. Socrates went as far as to say that the unexamined life is not even worth living. I did a Google search of the phrase "Why are we here?" and the results were many different websites expounding on the meaning of life. The question of our purpose as a species has been around for nearly as long as man has been here and there are many different schools of thought. One such man who sought to know himself in the hopes of discovering meaning in his existence was the author of the Book of Ecclesiastes.

In this book, we have Solomon, one of the wisest, richest, and most powerful men to have ever lived, ruminating on earthly life and concluding that it is all just vanity. Life is vanity because, in a sense, our meaning has been deferred. There is no meaning now, only preparation for the time when there will be meaning. God created man to be in a state of fellowship with Him, to enjoy us and for us to enjoy Him. He created us to enjoy and care for each other, and to take pride in our dominion over the world and the product of our labor that results from that dominion. Therein lay our original meaning: to love God and to enjoy all of His creation. However, when we sinned, we lost that meaning. There was now enmity between God and us. Our relationships with each other became strained. Our dominion of the world became work, work that is often fruitless.

This is the world that Solomon surveys and continually calls it vanity; all is vanity. The pursuit of knowledge, the fruit of our labor, the wine, women, and song of hedonism, it is all pointless. This is the result of our fall from grace: a world that in and of itself is devoid of meaning and purpose. Look all you want across all the corners of the world, the great philosophers, the scientists, all the great and wise men, they can tell you much about this world, but they can't give it meaning. The wisdom of this world cannot restore life to its own corpse.

So, is there hope? Is there a meaning? Solomon thought so. After ruminating far and wide about this world and the nature of his existence, the philosopher-king comes to this conclusion:

> *Let us hear the conclusion of the whole matter: Fear God, and keep His commandments: for this is the whole duty of man. For God shall bring every work into judgment, with every secret thing, whether it be good, or whether it be evil.*

Centuries later, another king would echo this sentiment. You should love the Lord your God, he would say, with all your heart, with all your soul, with your entire mind and with all your strength. Moreover, you should love your neighbor, which is all of mankind, as we love our very selves. Here is where we find our meaning. There are no commandments that are greater than this…this great directive of love. The meaning, then, gives us the purpose of communicating, not just love, but the greatest love, to all mankind. This is the Great Commission.

The Great Commission

In the military, to commission a battleship is to place it into active duty, to put it into battle. When an officer is commissioned, they are given authority by a sovereign power. These officers are given duties, responsibilities and power that they are obligated to use in service of the sovereign. As Christians, we also have been placed into active duty, on the front lines of the battle, with the following words from Christ recorded in the Gospel of Luke:

> *Then opened He their understanding, that they might understand the Scriptures, and said unto them, "Thus it is written, and thus it behooved Christ to suffer and to rise from the dead the third day, and that repentance and remission of sins should be preached in His name among all nations, beginning at Jerusalem.*

Read that passage carefully. It is not optional; it is a direct order. The version in Mark is even more direct: "Go ye into all the world, and preach the Gospel to every creature. He that believeth and is baptized shall be saved; but he that believeth not shall be damned." Again in the book of Acts: "ye shall be witnesses unto Me both in Jerusalem, and in all Judea and in Samaria, and unto the uttermost part of the earth." And in John: "Then said Jesus to them again, "Peace be unto you. As My Father hath sent Me, even so send I you." I do not see the chance here to "opt out." However, sadly many Americans do. In his book, *Futurecast*, George Barna notes that 49% of us feel that there is no responsibility to share one's religious beliefs with anyone else. The body of commissioned officers has been effectively cut in half by choice.

Talking to people about something as personal as our faith can be hard, even terrifying for some of us. Especially when you know that you are faced with a hostile audience, even if it is just an audience of one. Nevertheless, we have the prime directive of doing so. As I said earlier, one of the biggest barriers between non- believers and Jesus Christ, are Christians and our lives that are contradictory to the faith that we profess. One will never know how much easier and more fruitful our Great Commission might be if we were to simply be consistent. If we do, or condone, or tolerate that which our faith specifically preaches against, our efforts are already doomed to fail. To the unbelieving world, we are the face of Christ and if our actions, the words we use, the movies we watch, the music we listen to, are no different than anyone else's, we have already failed to live up to responsibility of the commission we have been tasked with by our Sovereign and have, therefore lost much of the power needed to carry out the mission. Our failure may very well have eternal consequences for those around us.

Too often our attitude can be, "I got mine; let the world worry about its own." Even if we do not explicitly make such a statement, that is how we live. We tend to think that we really worked at getting "ours." Or as if we deserved it more than everyone else did. Sometimes we seem like a parent telling a child to get a job in order to learn the value of a dollar; "why, in my day we were up at 4:30 in the morning, a Bible in one hand, a *Strong's Concordance* in the other…" But, it reality, it just that we allow ourselves to get too busy to even notice those around us. Our days are packed with the realities of this life: work, family, trying to find even a little "me time" in between coming home from work, helping kids with homework, doing the laundry, cooking, little league ballgames, birthday parties, and on and on… We are so wound up in just getting through our day that we never even notice the people around us unless they are facilitators or roadblocks to what ever our destination of the moment might be. To borrow a phrase from T.S. Eliot, "where is the Life we have lost in living?"

Love Wants to Share and Grow

It is easy to lose track of the simple fact that we are here to show one another love; to be each other's support, each other's shelter, each other's refuge from the negativity of the world that we so often create ourselves. We are a creation of love, we have been saved by love, every new morning that we are allowed to greet, every smile from our children, every touch from our lover, every little bit of hope that remains in us is a product of the love of God and it is our responsibility, our honor, to share that love with others in the same way that God has shared it with us. Love is a dynamic thing; it cannot be still, it cannot be quiet. It must be expressed. A love locked away, limited, is fated to darken and wither like a plucked rose. It can survive for a while, retain its vibrancy, its color, its aroma, but once its cut off from its source of nourishment, its fate is set. Therefore, we are to cultivate it, nourish it daily and, most of all set it out before the world, for all to see its beauty.

Love wants to share of itself; it wants to grow. God is not content to say, "Well, X% of mankind has sought me and shall enjoy an eternity in my presence. That's a pretty good haul." No, he wants us all to know Him. That is why He has tasked us with the job of being His envoys. Christ died so that ALL may be saved, not just an acceptable percentage. However, what we must not do is to become so satisfied with our own salvation that we choose to coast towards eternity. That is not love, it certainly is not indicative of someone filled with the spirit of God. His heart should be our heart; a heart that desires that all be saved. Love reaches out to all and not just to those we deem as worthy, love is tireless unto the end, it is hopeful even when there is no earthly reason to hope, it is a reason to praise even in the darkest of nights, it is a reason to look up when the whole world seems to be dragging us down. Love, when given, grows exponentially. The smallest seed can become a great abundance. This is our task: to plant the seed so that He may reap the harvest.

A Life More Abundant

> *I am come that they might have life, and that they might have it more abundantly – John 10:10*

When most of us consider this scripture, of life more abundant, we tend to think of material things. We often take this to mean that a life more abundant is one of a wealth, one of comfort. Perhaps this is true. There are certainly plenty of pastors who seem to base their entire ministry around that interpretation. Just turn on the television o n a Sunday morning o r c h e c k o u t the bookstores and you will see what I mean. The Prophets of Profit, with an audience comprised largely of poor, urban, and minority devotees, seem to be using faith as a means to reach the American Dream. It's "Christ as Business Model" theology, being taught by pastors in suits that cost more than many in their audience make in a week, wearing jewelry that their audience couldn't buy with even a month's salary. God save us from ourselves.

When you consider that even the poorest of Americans has a standard of living that is unimaginable in Biblical times to all but the likes of King Solomon, one has to wonder what Christ's contemporaries would think about our incessant pleas for more. No, perhaps having life and having it more abundantly means something more than acquiring another car or satellite TV.

Perhaps it is not an abundance of things in our life, but an abundance of life itself, with which we should be concerned. How could life be more abundant than that of an eternity in the presence of God? Perhaps we accept the life of abundance here, the terms are agreed upon with us giving very little in return, but it is acquired only when we see the guarantor face-to-face. An eternal life in the presence of Jesus Christ, life more abundant!

Oh, I am sure that some of that abundance is accessible here and now, and maybe some of it is material things, but what of an abundance of faith, of love, of the presence of God in your life. Because, in the end, aren't those the things that we need the most? Aren't those the things that, if missing from your life, will lead you down the path of destruction? Lack of material things does not cause crime; growing up in a house devoid of faith, of love, of the presence of God can. Living on a modest means does not cause the sort of spiraling depression that so often ends in alcoholism, drug abuse, and even suicide. A life robbed of its meaning, without hope, with no future often does. Poverty does not lead to teenage pregnancy, overflowing prisons, no-fault divorces, a culture coarsened to the point that pre-teens are sexualized on television, women are degraded matter-of-factly in music, and mainstream cinema makes it a habit of mocking the values for which the church should stand and defend. But, a deficit of faith will leave you dreading every morning that you wake up to your own existence: an existence that you numb with alcohol, drugs, sexual "hook-ups," anything to turn off your life, if only for a little while.

A modest income does not mean a broken home, but a home without love is virtually doomed. Generations tend to repeat the same mistakes of the previous one, and a child who sees and suffers abuse in the home, is likely to carry those traits into their own relationships. If divorce seemed like the best solution for mom and dad, there is no reason why I should fight for my marriage, is there? A child that grows up subjected to dad's temper and alcoholism and mom excusing his fits of rage, may never know a loving family environment of their own. By the time they are ready to marry, the cycle of abuse is already so ingrained in them that the odds of them having a normal, successful relationship are minimal.

Refer back to the FBI statistics that I quoted in the first chapter to see what a society that does not have an abundance of God looks like. In the absence of God, our conscience, the sense of right and wrong, atrophies. Every act, no matter how heinous, can be justified in our own minds, if given the right circumstances. Without God in the picture, those circumstances will always exist. Without God, all things are permissible.

Therefore, when we pray for life more abundant, perhaps we should consider asking for more faith to get us through the dark nights of the soul. I love the story in Matthew of the centurion who came to Jesus to ask that he heal his servant. Jesus offered to come to the centurion's house to heal the servant but the centurion said no, he was not worthy enough for Christ to come to his home, but he knew that all Jesus had to do was to say the word and his servant would be healed.   This man, this Roman soldier, had so much faith in Christ that he believed a mere word from Christ's mouth would heal his servant.   He didn't need proof or assurances;   he didn't even need to see it happen.   All he needed was for Christ to say it was so, and he knew that it would be so.

This was a Roman soldier, the occupying enemy of the Jewish people, but here he was, showing a faith in Christ that even Christ's own people did not have in him.   Jesus marveled at the faith of the centurion and declared it greater than that of any of the people of Israel, which would include his own disciples! Jesus then declared:

> *I say to you that many will come from the east and the west, and will take their places at the feast with Abraham, Isaac and Jacob in the kingdom of heaven.   But the subjects of the kingdom will be thrown outside, into the darkness, where there will be weeping and gnashing of teeth."*

This prophetic reference to the inclusion of the Gentiles (those from the east and west of Israel) thanks to their centurion-like faith is contrasted to the unbelieving people of Israel (the subjects of the kingdom). It is the abundance of faith that allows them a place at the feast with Abraham, Isaac and Jacob, not their credit score.

So, perhaps we should look at an abundant life as a promise of an abundance of life itself.   It's not about disposable income, what kind of vacation you can afford to take, or if your car is newer than your neighbor's car. An abundant life is a life with the gift of Christ himself. It is a life where his sacrifice removed the barriers between God and Man, tore the veil, and opened up the throne room of God to all who seek His presence. Isn't that a greater inheritance?

Epilogue

We live in an age of contradictions, one in which the life that God created is used as key evidence against His existence. The God of Abraham and Moses, who sent His son to die for us all, the very fount of love and hope, has been tried and found wanting, so we create our own deities, in our own images. We are a people who relegate Christ to the role of a motivational speaker and approach Scripture with scissors and a bottle of whiteout. Bloated with hubris and an overweening dedication to our Self, we recast God in our own image, the previous millennia of philosophy, science and the quest for knowledge having culminated in nothing more than a journey of self-discovery based upon the ramblings of some daytime television, self-help guru. We were given the key to the universe and were quite content to slip it in our back pocket and remain still, gazing into the Narcissistic pool of the Self until that is all that remains. Our age is that which the poet T.S. Eliot wrote of in "The Rock":

Endless invention, endless experiment,

Brings knowledge of motion, but not of stillness;

Knowledge of speech, but not of silence;

Knowledge of words, and ignorance of the Word.

All our knowledge brings us nearer to our ignorance,

All our ignorance brings us nearer to death,

But nearness to death no nearer to GOD.

Where is the Life we have lost in living?

Where is the wisdom we have lost in knowledge?

Where is the knowledge we have lost in information?

The cycles of Heaven in twenty centuries

Bring us farther from GOD and nearer to the Dust.

In the story of the unfaithful servant, Jesus tells us "unto whomsoever much is given, of him shall be much required." This should have a special meaning to those of us in the West and especially in the United States. I'm not talking about our wealth relative to the rest of the world, although that is a part of it. I am talking about our freedom, our liberty, and our ability to reach out to those who cannot reach out to us. Much has been given to us; we can worship freely, openly. We can discuss our faith publicly.

Much of the world does not have that luxury. For nearly 200 years, the United States and most of the Western world has been uniquely situated to spread the gospel; we have been God's megaphone to a world desperately in need of the Good News. We have been a tool, a medium for the message. Much as the scholarship of ancient Greece and the infrastructure of the Roman Empire facilitated the spread of early Christianity, the unprecedented prosperity and influence of the West has been used by God to reach out to the rest of the world. But, has the salt lost its savor? According to Talbot School of Theology's Dr. William Lane Craig, nearly 2/3 of all evangelicals live in the Third World. By 1991, the number of evangelicals living in Asia surpassed the number living in the entire Western world. Based upon the numbers, Christianity, rather than being a Western, white religion, is an Asian religion. Have we exhausted our usefulness? Has the torched been passed on as we g o the way of an increasingly secular, postmodern Europe? What has historically happened to civilizations that have lost their willingness to be God's messengers, to live according to His standards? Thomas Jefferson fully understood the consequences of a nation falling away from God when he said, "I tremble for my country when I recall that God is just; and that His justice will not sleep forever." The wrath of God is a terrible thing to contemplate, but contemplate it we must. Everyday it becomes more evident that we flirting wih being abandoned to reap the fruits of our disobedience. Romans 1:18-32 looks as if it could have been written with 21st century America in mind:

"…men who suppress the truth in unrighteousness."

"…though they knew God, they did not honor Him as God or give thanks."

"…professing to be wise, they became fools, and exchanged the glory of the incorruptible God for an image in the form of corruptible man and of birds and four-footed animals and crawling creatures."

"…they exchanged the truth of God for a lie, and worshiped and served the creature rather than the Creator."

"…the men abandoned the natural function of the woman and burned in their desire toward one another, men with men committing indecent acts and receiving in their own persons the due penalty of their error."

"…God gave them over to a depraved mind, to do those things which are not proper,

 being filled with all unrighteousness, wickedness, greed, evil; full of envy, murder, strife, deceit, malice; they are gossips, slanderers, haters of God, insolent, arrogant, boastful, inventors of evil, disobedient to parents, without understanding, untrustworthy, unloving, unmerciful."

"…although they know the ordinance of God, that those who practice such things are worthy of death, they not only do the same, but also give hearty approval to those who practice them."

For all this, God gave them over, abandoned them, as He did the Northern Kingdom of Israel, as He is doing to the Kingdom of the United States; abandoned them to wallow in the filth that they chose to worship in place of God.

We are not a Christian nation, perhaps we never really were. At best, we are a post-Christian nation, and we are very quickly becoming a post-modern nation. What we were is of little concern at this point. Yesterday is over; we must contend with today. It does us no good to fret and wring our hands over which Founding Father was a Christian or a deist or an atheist. We cannot change history and it certainly should not be our goal to rewrite it. Granted, we should know our own history and defend it, but we also must simply accept it for what it was and move on.

Rather, the problem that we face is that the character of a nation is nothing more than the character of its people. So, what is the character of our nation today? In a nation in which 75% of us claim to be Christians, are we creating a Christian character for our nation, or one that will result in God's abandonment wrath? What sort of nation will we leave for our children tomorrow? Our every choice and action today, or lack thereof, is building the foundation for tomorrow. What sort of tomorrow will it be? Is it a tomorrow that we would even want for our selves, let alone our children?

We have the responsibility of creating tomorrow simply because we exist. There is no escaping it and no way out.

We can rise to it or we can shirk it and, by default, leave a world of chaos and hate in our apathetic wake.

The choice is a simple one: to stand with Jesus or to stand alone and fall. Just know one thing, if you do choose to go it alone, or if you choose Jesus and only do it as a half-measure, as a DMV Christian, your failure will echo through the following generations and you will drag many down with you, strangers, friends, your children. Your example may be their fate. So, choose well.

Works Cited

1) Russell, Bertrand. God and Religion, Amherst: Prometheus Books, 1986

2) "How Religious is Your State?" The Pew Forum on Religion and Public Life. 21 Dec. 2009. Pew Research Center. 25 Oct. 2011. http://pewforum.org/How-Religious-Is-Your-State-.aspx

3) "Crime in the United States." Sept. 2010. United States Department of Justice. 25 Oct. 2011. http://www2.fbi.gov/ucr/cius2009/data/table_02.html

4) Barna, George. Futurecast, Austin: Tyndale, 2011.

5) "Statement of Faith." National Association of Evangelicals. 2009. National Association of Evangelicals. 25 Oct. 2011.

http://www.nae.net/about-us/statement-of-faith

6) Schroeder, Gerald. Genesis and the Big Bang: The Discovery of Harmony Between modern Science and the Bible. New York: Bantam, 1990.

Hawking, Stephen. A Brief History of Time. New

York: Bantam, 1996.

7) Schaefer, Henry F., Science and Christianity:

Conflict or Coherence. Watkinsville, GA: The

Apollos Trust, 2003

8) "Nicholas Copernicus." Calendars through the

Ages. 2008. 25 Oct. 2011.

http://www.webexhibits.org/calendars/year-text-

Copernicus.html

9) Hooper, Simon. "The Rise of the New Atheists."

9, Nov. 2006. CNN. 25 Oct. 2011.

http://www.cnn.com/2006/WORLD/europe/11/08/a

theism.feature/index.html.

10) Dawkins, Richard. The God Delusion. New York:

First Mariner Books, 2006.

11) Harris, Sam. Letter to a Christian Nation. New

York: Random House, 2008.

12) Ibid

13) Dawkins, Richard. The God Delusion. New York:

First Mariner Books, 2006.

14) Dietrich Bonhoeffer, *Letters and Papers from Prison*, New York: Simon & Schuster, 1997) "Letter to Eberhard Bethge", 29 May 1944

15) Hobbes, Thomas. Leviathan. Oxford: Oxford University Press, 2008.

16) Lewis, C.S. Mere Christianity. New York: Harper Collins, 2001.

17) Greene, Richard Allen. "Religious Belief is Human Nature, Huge New Study Claims." 12 May 2005. CNN. 25 Oct. 2011. http://religion.blogs.cnn.com/2011/05/12/religious-belief-is-human-nature-huge-new-study-claims/

18) Law, William. A Serious Call to a Devout and Holy Life. Alachua: Bridge-Logos, 2008.

19) Wells, Amos R. "You Who Like to Play at Bible." The Collected Poems of Amos R. Wells. The Christian Endeavor World. 1921.

20) Lewis. C.S. "The Problem of Praise in the Psalms." Reflections on the Psalms. New York: Harcourt, Brace and World, 1958.

New Testament Christian. 2006. 25, Oct. 2011.

http://www.new-testament-

christian.com/conscience.html

21) "Repentance in Judaism." Wikipedia. 02, Sept.

2011. Wikimedia Foundation, Inc. 25 Oct. 2011.

http://en.wikipedia.org/wiki/Repentance_in_Judais

m#The_end_of_sacrifices

22) Dostoevsky, Fyodor. The Brothers Karamazov.

Hertfordshire: Wordsworth Editions, 2007.

23) Sartre, Jean Paul. "Existentialism is a

Humanism." Existentialism from Dostoevsky to

Sartre. Meridian Publishing Company. 1989.

24) Lewis, C.S. Mere Christianity. New York: Harper

Collins, 2001.

25) Eliot, T.S. "The Rock." Wisdom Portal. Ed. Peter

Y. Chou. 25 Oct. 2011.

http://www.wisdomportal.com/Technology/TSEliot-

TheRock.html

26) Ibid

27) Lane, William Craig. "Subject: Molinism, the

Unevangelized and Cultural Chauvinism."

Reasonable Faith with William Lane Craig. 25

Oct. 2011.

http://www.reasonablefaith.org/site/News2?page=

NewsArticle&id=5681